MEMOIR OF CATHARINE BROWN,

A CHRISTIAN INDIAN OF THE CHEROKEE NATION

RUFUS ANDERSON, A.M.

Assistant Secretary of the American Board of Commissioners for Foreign Missions

Our Christian Heritage Foundation

Copyright © 2012 Our Christian Heritage Foundation

All rights reserved.

ISBN-10: 0615736963
ISBN-13: 978-0615736969

This book is Volume 2 of Our Christian Heritage Foundation's Historical Reprints Series
Also Available from Our Christian Heritage Foundation:
The Religion that Shaped America, Dr. Byron Perrine, Editor.
Emerson's Evangelical Primer, Vol. 1 of Our Christian Heritage Foundation's Historical Reprints Series.

PREFACE FROM THE 1827 EDITION

This Memoir was commenced as a biographical article for the Missionary Herald. In its progress, however, the materials were found to be so abundant, as to suggest the inquiry, whether a distinct publication were not expedient.

Such a publication being advised, by the Prudential Committee of the Board of Missions, it is respectfully offered to those who feel interested in the success of missionary efforts.

The author is not conscious of having exaggerated a single fact, nor of having made a single statement not drawn from authentic documents. His object has been to give a plain and true exhibition of the life and character of a very interesting convert from heathenism.

The hope is cherished, that this little volume will augment the courage, animate the zeal, and invigorate the efforts, of the friends of missions, in their benevolent attempts to send the Gospel of Jesus Christ to all nations.

Missionary Room,
Boston, Mass. Dec. 1824

ACKNOWLEDGMENTS

This book has been transcribed from the Third Edition of Memoir of Catharine Brown, A Christian Indian of the Cherokee Nation by Rufus Anderson, A.M., originally published in Cincinnati by Morgan, Fisher and L'Hommedieu in 1827.

THIS EDITION DEDICATED TO

The Teachers, Staff and Students
of Christian Boarding Schools
Everywhere

CONTENTS

1   Her History Until She Entered the Mission School At Brainerd   1

2   From Her Entering The School At Brainerd, Until Her Removal By Her Parents   9

3   From Her Return To Brainerd, Until She Takes Charge Of A School At Creek-Path   33

4   From Her Taking Charge Of A School At Creek-Path, Until Her Sickness   55

5   Her Sickness And Death   96

6   Her Character   115

CHAPTER 1.
HER HISTORY UNTIL SHE ENTERED THE MISSION SCHOOL AT BRAINERD

Catharine Brown was born about the year 1800. The place of her nativity was a beautiful plain, covered with tall forest trees, in a part of the country belonging to the Cherokee Indians, which is now called Wills-Valley, and lies within the chartered limits of the state of Alabama. It is between the Raccoon and Lookout mountains, twenty-five miles south-east of the Tennessee river. David, the brother of Catharine, says that the name, by which the place is known among his countrymen, is *Tsu sau-ya-sah,* or *the ruins of a great city.* But, if such ruins ever existed, all traces of them have long since disappeared.

The Indian name of Catharine's father, is *Yau-nu-gung-yah-ski,* which signifies *the drowned by a bear.* He is, however, known among the whites by the name of *John Brown.* The Cherokee name of her mother is *Tsa-luh*. The whites call her *Sarah*.

Neither of Catharine's parents understand the English language. They are now about sixty years of age. Since the decease of the daughter, whose history and character are to form the subject of this memoir, they have removed beyond the Mississippi river to the Arkansas Territory, whither a part of the Cherokee nation of Indians have emigrated, within the last fifteen or twenty years.*

---

*A more particular account of the family of Catharine, may be acceptable to the reader.

Mr. John Brown was the son of a man named Brown who, has long been dead. It is not known whether he was a white man, or partly Indian. The mother of Mr. Brown was a "full-blooded" Cherokee. So, also, was the mother of Mrs. Brown; but her father was white. Catharine's parents were brought up like others of their nation;--no better acquainted with the language, religion, manners, or customs of the white people.

Mr. Brown had three wives. The first had two children, neither of whom are living. One of these children became a man of much distinction. In the Creek war he had the title of Colonal, as he commanded a large number of Cherokees, who made a part of the army under Gen. Jackson. He was severely wounded at the battle of the Horseshoe; but recovered, and died subsequently of a fever, or consumption. He is said to have possessed uncommon powers of mind, and to have exerted much influence among the people. He is familiarly referred to by the name of Col. Dick Brown.

The children of Sarah, the second and present wife of Mr. Brown; were John, who died in the Christian faith, February, 1822,

Mr. Brown is represented as possessing a mind more than commonly discerning; yet as having, when the missionaries first saw him, but few ideas on the subject of religion. He believed in a Supreme Being, the author of the visible creation, and that there is a state of rewards and punishments after the present life; and appeared

---

leaving a widow, Susannah who is a professor of religion; Catharine, the subject of this memoir; and David, of whose piety hopes have been entertained for almost five years.

The children of the third wife, named Wattee, or Betsy, who, for some years has been living in the Arkansas Territory, are Polly (or Mrs. Gilbreth), Alexander, Susan, and Edmund. Polly and Susan are esteemed pious.

Sarah and Betsy lived with Mr. Brown, at the same time. But some difficulty arising, the latter separated from him.

Sarah was the wife of a man named Weber, before she married Mr. Brown. The children by this marriage, are Betsy, (now Mrs. Looney,) a professor of religion, and Walter, called Col. Webber. He was at Washington city, about two years since, and possesses a handsome property. These children were quite young when their father died. Col. Weber is now about thirty-five years old.

It appears, therefore, that of Mr. Brown's family no less than nine have become hopefully pious, within the last seven years, viz: Mr. and Mrs. Brown, John, Catharine, David, Polly, Susan, Susannah, and Mrs. Looney.

The reader will apt to infer, when he sees individuals called by names and titles, with which he is familiar, that they are very much like other individuals whom he has known under similar titles, in short, that they are civilized and intelligent persons. Such and inference, however, is not warranted. The mere possession of an English name, in an Indian country, is no evidence that the person thus distinguished is able to speak the English language, much less that his habits are those of civilized life, or that his mind has been

conscious that there were things implied in this short creed, of which he had no distinct apprehension; such was the character of the Supreme Being, the nature of the rewards and punishments, and the manner in which the one was obtained, and the other avoided. He seemed to have no notion of forgiveness of sin upon any terms. When told of these things, he said he had never heard of them before.

Concerning the *mother*, less is known to the writer of this memoir. Her religious knowledge, if equal to that of her husband, did not probably exceed it. She is represented as having been more attentive to neatness and good order, in the internal arrangements of the family, and more conversant with the duties of domestic life, than her countrywomen generally.

Ignorant s were the parents of Catharine, on the most important subjects, they belonged to the more intelligent class of their people. Till within

---

in any degree cultivated.

As to the military titles of captain, major, colonial, and even general, they are conferred as a matter of courtesy, in consequence of some sort of undefined authority, which is exercised over others, and which is supposed to bear some distant analogy to the authority, implied in those titles among us. Of course, the titles are conferred by the whites in some instances, when Indian auxiliaries have been employed in active warfare, by European governments, or by the United States, individuals may have received regular commission. Mr. Brown and his son John, were both denominated Captain.

a few years, the Cherokees had scarcely begun to feel an impulse towards civilization. Indeed, as a nation, they were almost entirely destitute of the means of intellectual or moral culture. In a very few instances, a youth was sent to school in the white settlements, bordering on the Indian territory; and still more rarely, perhaps, an outcast from civilized society would undertake for a short time, and from interested, and probably sinister motives, to instruct among the natives. In 1801, a Moravian mission was established at what is now called Spring-place, and one or two excellent men have, since that period, resided there. But their means having been limited, their influence could not be extensive. Very commendable exertions, in support of a school among the Cherokees, were also made, for a few years subsequent to 1803, by the Rev. Gideon Blackburn.

Excepting these efforts, there was, until the year 1816, nothing done for the Cherokees by the Christian church, nothing by the civilized world. They inhabited a country, which is described as being susceptible of the highest cultivation: but most imperfect was their agriculture. They possessed a language, that is said to be more precise and powerful, than many, into which learning has poured richness of thought, or genius breathed the enchantments of fancy and eloquence: but they had no literature. Not a book existed in the language. The fountains of knowledge were unopened. The mind made no progress.

After these statements, the reader will be prepared to credit what will be said, in the progress of this memoir, respecting Catharine's intellectual condition, when she first came under the care of the missionaries.

It is pleasing to observe here, that her moral character was ever irreproachable. This is remarkable, considering the looseness of manners then prevalent among the females of her nation, and the temptations to which she was exposed, when, during the war with the Creek Indians the army of the United States was stationed near her father's residence. Were it proper to narrate some well authenticated facts, with reference to this part of her history, the mind of the reader would be filled with admiration of her heroic virtue, as well as of the protecting care of Providence. Once she even forsook her home, and fled into the wild forest, to preserve her character unsullied.*

These occurrences took place before the establishment of a school at Brainerd, while Catharine was young, ignorant of the world, with

---

*"I was pleased to find," says a friend, "that Gen. Jackson, (who commanded in the war with the Creeks,) had a high opinion of Catharine. In the course of our conversation he remarked, "she was a woman of Roman virtue, and above suspicion."

no clear views of morality, and without the knowledge and love of God. Strange that so strong a sense of character should then have influenced her resolutions! But she was a chosen vessel of mercy, and a hand, which she did not then know, was doubtless extended for her preservation.

Early in the autumn of 1816, a missionary, sent by the American Board of Commissioners for Foreign Missions, made his appearance in a general Council of the Cherokees, and offered to establish schools among them. His offer was favorably received. After consultation, a principal chief came forward, took him by the hand, and said: "You have appeared in our full Council. We have listened to what you have said, and understand it. We are glad to see you. We wish to have the schools established, and hope they will be of great advantage to the nation." This missionary was the Rev. Cyrus Kingsbury, who, after commencing the first establishment of the Board among the Cherokees, took up his residence among the Choctaws, was the chief agent in forming the stations of Elliot and Mayhew, and is now the superintendent of the Choctaw mission.

The place selected for the first school, was then called Chichamaugah; but it subsequently received the name of Brainerd, in memory of David Brainerd, that devoted friend and benefactor of the American Indians, who stands preeminent among modern missionaries.* Early in the follow spring, Mr. Moody Hall and Mr. Loring S. Williams, with their wives, arrived as assistant missionaries; and, soon after their arrival, a school was opened, with fair prospects of success.

Information of these proceedings soon spread through the nation. It came to the ears of Catharine, then living at the distance of a hundred miles, and excited in her a desire to attend the school. She besought her parents to send her, and they granted her request. Accordingly, on the 9th of July, 1817, when she was about seventeen or eighteen years of age, she became a member of the missionary school at Brainerd.

---

*Brainerd is situated within the chartered limits of Tennessee, on the Chickamaugah creek; two miles north of the line of Georgia; seven miles south east of Tennessee river; two hundred and fifty north-west of Augusta in Geo.; one hundred and fifty south east of Nashville, and one hundred and ten south-west of Knoxville, both in Tennessee.

CHAPTER 2.
FROM HER ENTERING THE SCHOOL AT BRAINERD, UNTIL HER REMOVAL BY HER PARENTS

Thus was Catharine brought, for the first time, within the sphere of Christian instruction. Even then she was an interesting girl: her complexion blooming; her features comely; her person erect, and of the middle stature; her manners easy; her demeanor modest and prepossessing.

"It was, however, manifest" says Mr. Kingsbury, "that, with all her gentleness and apparent modesty, she had a high opinion of herself, and was fond of displaying the clothing and ornaments in which she was arrayed. At our first interview, I was impressed with the idea, that her feelings would not easily yield to the discipline of our schools, especially to that part of it, which requires manual labor of the scholars. This objection I freely stated to her, and requested that, if she felt any difficulty on the subject, she would seek admission to some other school. She replied, that she had no objection to our regulations. I advised her to take the subject into consideration, and to obtain what information she could, relative to the treatment of the scholars, and if she then felt a desire to become a member of the school, we would receive her.

She joined the school, and the event has shown, that it was of the Lord, to the end that his name might be glorified. I have often reflected, with adoring gratitude and thankfulness, on the good providence which conducted that interesting young female to Brainerd, and which guided her inquiring and anxious mind to the Savior of sinners.

Some time before this, it is not known precisely how long, while residing at the house of a Cherokee friend, she had learned to converse in the English language on common subjects, and to read words of one syllable. These acquisitions, which were of no particular service at the time they were made, are to be noticed with gratitude to God, as the probable means of leading her to Brainerd. They excited desires, which she could gratify nowhere else.

Her teachers declare, that, from her first admission to the school, she was attentive to her learning, industrious in her habits, and remarkably correct in her deportment. From reading words of one syllable, she was able, in sixty days, to read the bible intelligibly, and, in ninety days, could read as well as most persons of common education. After writing over four sheets of paper, she could us the pen with accuracy and neatness, even without a copy.

From the testimony of different persons it appears, that, when she entered the school, her knowledge on religious subjects was exceedingly vague and defective. Her ideas of God extended little further than the contemplation of him as a great Being, existing somewhere in the sky; and her conceptions of a future state were quite undefined. Of the Savior of the world, she had no knowledge. She supposed that the Cherokees were a different race from the whites, and therefore had no concern in the white people's religion; and it was some time before she could be convinced, that Jesus Christ came into the world to die for the Cherokees. She has been known, also, to remark, subsequently to her conversion, that, when she was first conversed with in regard to religion, she was much afraid; for she thought Christians could have no pleasure in this world, and that, if she became religious, she too should be rendered unhappy. How much her opinions and sentiments on this subject were, in a short time, changed will abundantly appear as we proceed.

That the reader may be duly sensible of the singleness of heart and Christian devotedness of the men, under whose instruction this interesting female had placed herself, he is informed, that, not long after her introduction to them, they adopted the following resolution, which develops an economical principle, carried through all the missions to the Indians, under the direction of the American Board of Commissioners for Foreign Missions:

"That, as God in his providence has called us to labor in the great and good work of building up his kingdom among the Aborigines of this country, a work peculiarly arduous, and which will be attended with much expense; and above all, considering that we have solemnly devoted ourselves, and all that we have, to the prosecution of this work; we declare it to be our cordial, deliberate, and fixed resolution, that, so far as it respects our future labors, or any compensation for them, we will have no private interests distinct from the great interests of this institution; and, that if it meets the views of the Prudential Committee, we will receive no other compensation for our services, than a comfortable supply of food and clothing for ourselves and families, and such necessary expenses as our peculiar circumstances may require; observing at all times that frugality and economy, which our duty to the Christian public and the great Head of the Church demands."

Catharine had been in the school but a very few months, before divine truth began to exert an influence upon her mind. This was manifested by a tenderness of spirit, and an increased desire to become acquainted with the Christian religion. The same effects were also observed, at the same time, in two or three other Cherokees.

She did not seem to be greatly influenced by a fear of the punishment the punishment threatened against sin. Her chief object of solicitude seemed rather to be, that she might know the will of God, and do it. She sought the kingdom of heaven with great earnestness, spent much time in reading the Scriptures, singing and prayer, and was often affected to tears.

In December, 1817, she indulged a hope, that she had been pardoned and accepted, through the Lord Jesus Christ. And it is no small proof of the excellent practical tendency of her religion, that, of her own accord, she very soon began to pray with her associates, and to assist in teaching the Lord's Prayer and the catechism to the young girls in the school.

The Rev. William Chamberlain, now residing at the missionary station called Willstown, not far from the place of her nativity, states, that her desires for the salvation of her people, were now strong and ardent. For them she wept and prayed, in secret places, and in the company of her female friends at their weekly prayer-meetings.

Among the rest, the case of her brother David, then on the Arkansas river, was especially interesting. One morning, having retired to the neighboring woods for devotion, she became so deeply engaged in prayer for this dear brother, that the time passed insensibly, and she remained in her sacred retreat till the sun was near setting. She had been favored with unusual nearness of access to her heavenly Father, and returned home with an humble confidence, that he would fully answer her prayers. After David had gone to New-England to complete his education, having previously given satisfactory evidence of piety, she related these facts to a confidential friend, and said she wished to remember them with gratitude.

At the commencement of the year 1818, an event occurred, which showed how much Catharine was attached to the society and the privileges enjoyed at Brainerd. Her father, designing to remove with his family beyond the Mississippi river, came to take her from the school.

The prospect of a separation was equally painful to Catharine and to the missionaries. They regarded her as the first fruit of their missionary labors, and loved her, as well on that account, as on account of her pious and amiable conduct.— On her part, there was not less affection; and besides, she felt herself too weak to leave the society of God's people, and go into the howling wilderness alone.

"Perhaps," said her teachers and spiritual guides, "the Lord is taking her from us, that she may be more useful in promoting his cause in some other place."

We shall see, ere long, that they ultimately found occasion to give praise to God, not only on account of the brief separation, which now took place, but also for the more painful separation, which happened in this latter part of the same year.

Catharine desired to receive, before her departure, the seal of the covenant of grace, in the holy ordinance of baptism. As no reasonable doubt could be entertained of her piety, this request was cheerfully granted. On the 25th of January, Mr. Kingsbury preached from Gal 3:28, on the fellowship of those, who are in Christ, of whatever color, or nation. After the sermon and a prayer, the sacred ordinance was administered, in the presence of a large and solemn assembly, to the deeply affected convert.

She was the first Indian baptized by the missionaries of the Board. This event occurred about eight months after the opening of the school at Brainerd. Since then, about one hundred adult Cherokees have received the same ordinance preparatory to admission to the visible church.

The month of February was spent by Catharine at her father's house. But circumstances prevented the immediate removal of his parents, and she was permitted to revisit Brainerd for the purpose of spending a few months more on that hallowed ground.

She had been closely questioned, while at home, by some irreligious white people, with respect to her religious faith. They endeavored, though in vain, to perplex her mind, by objections against the Scriptures. But her parents were pleased that she had learned so many good things, and expressed a desire to be themselves instructed.

Her return furnished an opportunity to admit her to full communion in the visible Church of Christ; which was done on the 29th of March, about two months after her baptism, when she, with others, ratified a solemn covenant with the Most High, at the sacramental table. Seven of the communicants were Cherokees.

There is reason to believe, that some of the bystanders had no small desire to be with the little company, which commemorated the love of Jesus, particularly one negro woman. This person, being asked how she felt on that occasion, replied, "I felt as if that (meaning the communicants,) was my company, and that they had left me alone in the wicked world." "Our red brethren and sisters," say the missionaries, "declared, that their joys, while at the table, exceeded everything they had before conceived."

It has not been common for missionary stations among Pagans, to be favored so early, as was Brainerd, with the converting influences of the Spirit of God. Generally, in these latter days, the faith and patience of a missionary, under such circumstances, have been considerably tried, before he has seen the fruits of his labors; to be a harvest amply compensating him for all his toils. But among those Indians of North America, who have not incorporated the worst vices of civilized life with their own, the preacher of the Gospel has some peculiar advantages. They possess not, as do most heathen nations, a complicated system of false religion, transmitted before the Gospel can prevail. They are, to a great extent, "without a sacrifice, and without an image, and without an ephod, and without a teraphim." There is scarcely anything among the Indians themselves, to oppose the prevalence of the Gospel, except their unfortified ignorance and depravity. The greatest obstacles to missionary success among them, arise from a foreign influence, industriously, and sometimes, powerfully exerted.

In May, Jeremiah Evarts, Esq., at that time Treasurer of the American Board of

Commissioners for Foreign Missions, arrived at Brainerd, on a visit of inspection and superintendence. By extracting two or three passages from a letter, which he then wrote to Dr. Worcester, Corresponding Secretary of the Board, the reader will have an interesting view of the internal economy of the missionary establishment, with which Catharine was connected.

"It was on Friday evening, the 8th inst., just after sun-set," says Mr. Evarts, "that I alighted at the mission-house. The path, which leads to it from the main-road, passes through an open wood, which is extremely beautiful at this season of the year. The mild radiance of the setting sun, the unbroken solitude of the wilderness, the pleasantness of the forest with all its springing and blossoming vegetation, the object of my journey, and the nature and design of the institution, which I was about to visit, conspired to render the scene solemn and interest, and to fill the mind with tender emotions.

"Early in the evening, the children of the school, being informed that one of their northern friends, whom they had been expecting, had arrived, eagerly assembled in the hall, and were drawn up in ranks and particularly introduced. They are neither shy nor forward in their manners. To a stranger they appear not less interesting than other children of the same age; but, if he considers their circumstances and prospects, incomparably more so.

"At evening prayers, I was forcibly struck with the stillness, order, and decorum of the children, and with the solemnity of the family worship. A portion of Scripture was read, with Scott's practical observations; a hymn was sung, in which a large portion of the children united, and Mr. Hoyt led the devotions of the numerous family. If all the members of the Board could hear the prayers which are daily offered in their behalf at this station, (and I presume at all others under their superintendence,) and if all patrons and contributors could hear the thanks, which are returned to God for their liberality; and especially if they could see a large circle of children, lately rescued from Heathenism, kneeling with apparent seriousness, and engaging in the solemnities of Christian worship, one of them, [Catharine Brown] already a hopeful convert, and others thoughtful and inquiring;--if all these things could be seen, one may safely predict, that the exertions and sacrifices of the friends of missions would be increased four-fold. These things are not the less real, however, because they cannot be seen by every friend to the cause."

The Rev. Ard Hoyt, mentioned in the above extracts, joined the mission in the January preceding, and in June succeeded Mr. Kingsbury as superintendent of the Cherokee mission, the latter having removed to the Choctaw nation.

A further extract from the letter of Mr. Evarts will not only confirm much, that has already been said respecting Catharine, but will add some other particulars.

" Her parents are half-breeds, who have never learnt to speak English; yet if you were to see her at a boarding-school in New-England, as she ordinarily appears here, you would not distinguish her from well educated females of the same age, either by her complexion, features, dress, pronunciation or manners. If your attention were directed to her particularly, you would notice amore than ordinary modesty and reserve. If you were to see her in a religious meeting of pious females, you would not distinguish her, unless by her more than common simplicity and humility. When she joined the school in July last, (having come more than 100 miles for that sole purpose,) she could read in syllables of three letters, and was seventeen years old. From her superior manners and comely person she had probably attracted more attention, than any other female in the nation. She was vain, and excessively fond of dress, wearing a profusion of ornaments in her ears. She can now read well in the Bible, is fond of reading other books, and has been particularly pleased with the Memoirs of Mrs. Newell. Last fall she became serious, is believed to have experienced religion in the course of the autumn, and was baptized in January. Since that time, she has been constantly in the family, and all the female members of it have the most intimate knowledge of her conduct, and receive a frank disclosure of her feelings. It is their unanimous opinion, that she gives uncommon evidence of piety. At meetings for social prayer and religious improvement, held by them on every Thursday afternoon and Sabbath evening, Catharine prays in her turn, much to the gratification of her sisters in Christ. Her prayers are distinguished by great simplicity as to thought and language, and seem to be the filial aspirations of the devout child. Before Mrs. Chamberlain took charge of the girls, Catharine had, of her own accord, commenced evening prayer with them, just as they were retiring to rest. Sometime after this practice had been begun, it was discovered by one of the missionaries, who, happening to pass by the cabin where the girls lodge, overheard her pouring for her desires in very affecting and appropriate language. On being inquired of respecting it, she simply observed, that she had prayed with the girls, because she thought it was her duty. Yet this young woman whose conduct might now reprove many professing Christians, who have been instructed in religion from their infancy, only ten months ago had never heard of Jesus Christ, nor had a single thought whether the soul survived the body, or not. Since she became religious her trinkets have gradually disappeared, till only a single drop remains in each ear. On hearing that pious females have, in many instances, devoted their ornaments to the missionary cause, she has determined to devote hers also. In coming to this determination, she acted without influence from the advice of others."*

The time fled rapidly away, in pious employments and in Christian intercourse, and brought the long expected, much dreaded separation. It shall be described in the words of those, who, next to the interesting sufferer, felt it most.

" November 4. The parents of Catharine Brown called on us. They are on their way to the Agency. The old grey-headed man, with tears in his eyes, said he must go over the Mississippi. The white people would not suffer him to live here. They had stolen his cattle, horses, and hogs, until he had very little left. He expected to return from the Agency, in about ten days, and should then want Catharine to go home, and prepare to go with him to the Arkansas. We requested him

---

*Panoplist, vol. xiv. p. 344.

to leave his daughter with us yet a little while, and to go to the Arkansas without her; and we would soon send her to him, with much more knowledge than she now has. To this he would not consent; but signified a desire, that some of us would go along with him. It is a great trial to think of sending this dear sister away with only one year's tuition; but we fear she must go. The Lord can and will order otherwise, if, on the whole, it is for the best."

While her parents were gone to the Agency, Catharine made a farewell visit to Spring-place, the seat of the Moravian mission, about thirty-five miles from Brainerd. The feelings with which she parted from Mr. and Mrs. Gambold, the venerable missionaries there, were such as might be expected, from her high regard for their characters, and her prospect of never seeing them again. She returned to Brainerd on the 9th, and, on the 20th, the missionaries thus describe her removal.

"We had a very affecting scene in the departure of our sister Catharine. Her father and mother, returning from the Agency to go to the Arkansas, stopped yesterday for the purpose of taking her with them. She knew that she needed more information to be prepared to go alone into the wilderness, and entreated them to leave her with us a little longer. She is their only daughter,* and they would not consent on any terms. The struggle was very sever. She wept and prayed, and promised to come to them, as soon as she had finished her literary education, and acquired some further knowledge of the Christian religion. We engaged that she should be provided for while here, and assisted in going to them. Her mother said, she could not live, if Catharine would not now go with them. Catharine replied, that to her it would be more bitter than death to leave us, and go where there were no missionaries. Her father became impatient, and told her, if she would not mind him, and go with them now, he would disown her forever; but if she would now go, as soon as missionaries came to the Arkansas, (and he expected they would be there soon,) she might go and live with them as long as she pleased. He wished her to have more learning.

"Never before had this precious convert so severe a trial; and never, perhaps, did her graces shine so bright. She sought for nothing but to know her duty, and asked for a few minutes to be by herself undisturbed. She returned, and said she would go. After she had collected and put up her Clothing, the family were assembled, a parting

---

*Catharine had half-sisters, but was the only daughter of Mr. Brown by this marriage.

hymn was sung, and a prayer offered. With mingled emotions of joy and grief, we commended her to the grace of God, and they departed.

"Precious babe in Christ! A few months ago brought out of the dark wilderness; here illuminated by the word and Spirit of God; and now to be sent back into the dark and chilling shades of the forest, without one fellow traveler, with whom she can say, 'Our Father!' O ye, who with delight sit under the droppings of the sanctuary, and enjoy the communion of saints, remember Catherine in your prayers."

Thus was she removed from a place, endeared to her by some of the most pleasing associations of her life; and she departed, expecting to return no more. A day of sorrow must it have been to the members of the school, whose warmest attachment she had most effectually secured.
The chief consolation of her religious friends was, that the whole had been ordered by infinite Wisdom.

Early in the following month, information was received at Brainerd, that two children, who had been taken captive by the Cherokees form the Osage tribe of Indians, were in the lower part of the nation, and that one of them was supposed to be the sister of *Lydia Carter,* the interesting

"Little Osage Captive,"* who was then a member of the school. There being some reason to believe, that the man; in whose possession they were, might be induced to surrender them to the care of the missionaries, Mr. Hoyt, accompanied by his son, set out in quest of the unfortunate children. They travelled between two and three hundred miles, and encountered many hardships on their way. But though they found the children, and ascertained that one was indeed the sister of Lydia, they failed in their great object.

The man, who professed to be the owner of the children, would not relinquish them.**

The journey was not, however, in vain. Mr. Hoyt had the happiness of meeting with Catharine, at her father's house. This occurrence is thus noticed, in the journal of the mission

"In this tour, father Hoyt spent two nights and a day at the house of Catharine Brown's father. He was received with great cordiality by the whole family; and Catharine's joy was so great, that he says, 'I felt myself more than paid for the

---

*The little girl, a narrative of whom was published, in 1822 by the Rev. Elias Cornelius, Pastor of the Tabernacle Church, in Salem, MA.
**The girl was never obtained by the missionaries: but the boy was afterwards placed under their care, through the kindness of Colonel Meigs, the United States Agent, and through the benevolent enterprise of Mr. John Ross, a promising Cherokee young man. The boy was named Jon Osage Ross, in honor of Mr. Ross.

fatigues of the whole journey, by the first evening's opportunity.' Catharine said, it had been very dark times with her, since she left Brainerd. All around her were engaged for the riches and pleasures of the world; and because she could not unite with them as formerly, they were telling her, they supposed she thought herself very good now; that she expected heaven alone, & etc. Her greatest burden was, a fear that she should be drawn away from the right path, and at length be left to do like those around her."

While Mr. Hoyt was at her father's, he preached to a small audience of Cherokees, and one Indian woman was so much affected, that she wept during the whole service. After the departure of Mr. Hoyt, this woman sent for Catharine to read and explain the Bible to her, and to pray with her, which was repeatedly done. There is reason to believe, that a salutary and abiding impression was produced; for after Catharine's return to Brainerd, this poor female came all the way, a distance of more than a hundred miles, to hear, as she said, more about the Savior.

This chapter will be closed with two letters from Catharine to her friends, which are the earliest, of which her biographer has any knowledge. And this occasion is taken to remark, in this memoir, were written from the overflowing of her heart to persons with whom she was intimately acquainted, and hence with little study, or effort. The greater part of them have never before been published. They are generally copied from the originals, which are in a plain intelligible running hand, and the orthography is very seldom incorrect. Alterations in the sense, are never made; and corrections in the grammar, but rarely.

The first of the letters was written in the anticipation of her dreaded removal from her Christian friends, sixteen months from her first coming to Brainerd.

TO MRS. WILLIAMS AT ELLIOT.

Brainerd, Nov. 1, 1815.

My dearly beloved Sister,

I HAVE been wishing to write to you ever since you left us. You can hardly tell how my heart ached when I parted with you, expecting never to see you again in this world; but when I remembered that you were in the hands of the Lord, and that he would dispose of you as he pleased, it gave me joy equal to my sorrow.

O how I rejoiced, to think that you were going to carry the glad tidings of salvation to a people who had never heard of the dear Savior. I do hope and pray that the Lord will bless your labors among them, as he has here.

We were very lonesome when you left us,

especially at our prayer-meetings; but I hope our hearts were united in love. I was very sorry to hear that you were sick; but it rejoiced me to hear that you were recovering. O, my dear sister I will join with you in praising the Lord for his goodness in restoring you to health. I shall never forget you, or your kind endeavors to bring me to a knowledge of the Savior. Sometimes I feel the love of God shed abroad in my heart, and feel as if I should be willing to give up everything in this world to Christ. O how good it is to enjoy the presence of God; O that I might always enjoy it: but my heart is so band and so prone to leave the God I love, that I am afraid he will leave me. O my dear sister, do pray for me.

All the Cherokee brothers and sisters are well. Three of the scholars, viz: Lydia Lowry, and Alice and Peggy Wilson, we hope have obtained an interest in the Savior. Mr. Williams came here, and wished to take his daughters on a visit to Mr. Brown's. Nearly a week after, he sent word that he was not going to send them back to school again. We felt very much grieved to hear it.

I expect my father here every day. I do not know whether I shall go to the Arkansas, or not. I feel grieved when I think of leaving my Christian friends, and of going far from all religious people, into a wild howling wilderness, where no star shines to guide my wandering feet to the Babe of

Bethlehem; where no warning voice is heard to keep me in the straight path that leads to heaven. When I look to that dark region, I start back; but when I think of my two brothers there, and my dear parents, who are soon to go, I feel reluctant to stay behind, and leave them to perish alone.

Tell Mr. Williams and Mr. Kingsbury, that I remember them most affectionately, and also all the dear brothers and sisters at Yello Busha.

From your loving sister,
CATHARINE BROWN.

TO MR. AND MRS. CHAMBERLAIN, AT BRAINERD.

Fort Deposit, Dec. 12, 1818.
My dearly beloved Brother and Sister Chamberlain,

I JUST sit down to address you with my pen. But is this all? Am I so soon called to bid you adieu, and see your faces no more in this world? O my beloved friends, you know not the love I bear to that blessed spot, where I have spent so many happy hours with you; but it is past never to return.

Dear friends, I weep; my heart is full; tears flow from my eyes while I write; and why is it so? Do I murmur? God forbid. Ought I not to praise the Lord for what I have received, and trust him for everything? O yes, his ways are best, and he has graciously promised, that "all things shall work together for good to them that love him." But do I love him? Have I that love to him, which will enable me to keep all his commandments. Do I love him with all my heart? O that the Lord would search me, and lead me in the way of eternal life.

Since I left you, I have led a very lonesome life, and not heard the Gospel preached but once; that is when father Hoyt was here, and Milo. They came here on Tuesday evening. I was sitting in my room, and heard a knocking at the door. I bid them come in; and who but Milo appeared. I inquired if anybody was with him; he said his father was at the door. That rejoiced me very much, and I enjoyed myself very much while they were here. Blessed be God for sending them here to instruct us.

I am here among a wicked set of people, and never hear prayers, no any godly conversation. O my dear friends, pray for me: I hope you do. There is not a day passes but I think of you, and the kindness I received during the time I stayed with you. It is not my wish to go to the Arkansas; but God only knows what is best for me. I shall not attempt to tell you what I have felt since I left you, and the tears I have shed when I called to mind the happy moments we passed in singing the praises of God. However, I bear it as well as I possibly can, trusting in our dear Savior, who will never leave nor forsake them, that put their trust in him.

It may be possible, that I may see you once more; it would be a great happiness to me if I don't go to the Arkansas; perhaps I may; but if I should go, it is not likely we shall meet in this world again: but you will excuse me, for my heart feels what I cannot express with my pen. When I think and see the poor thoughtless Cherokees going on in sin, I cannot help blessing God, that he has led me in the right path to serve him.

Father will start to the Arkansas about some time after Christmas; but I am not certain that I shall go.

I thank you for your kind letters. Do write to me every opportunity.

I shall conclude with my love to all my brothers and sisters at Brainerd. Sister Flora, do kiss all the children for me. I shall expect letters from all the little girls. O may we meet at last in the kingdom of our blessed Savior, never more to part. Farewell, my dear brother and sister, farewell.

From you affectionate sister in Christ.
CATHARINE BROWN.

CHAPTER 3.
FROM HER RETURN TO BRAINERD, UNTIL SHE TAKES CHARGE OF A SCHOOL AT CREEK-PATH

Those, who will but observe, may often witness very affecting instances of the particular and merciful providence, which God exercises towards his children in this world. Both the removal and the return of Catharine may be regarded as such instances.

What was the precise influence upon her own character, of her being taken from Brainerd, cannot be determined; though there is little doubt but her faith and patience were by this means, increased. But the consequences of her removal to others, are more obvious, it led the way to the formation of schools, and to the stated preaching of the Gospel, at Creek-Path, the place of her father's residence, and to the hopeful conversion of nearly all her family; thus illustrating the maxim, that our greatest blessings may spring from our severest afflictions.

Her return was scarcely expected by the missionaries when, on the 23rd of May, 1819, her father brought her again to Brainerd, and committed her to their care, until her education should be completed, intending to remove immediately with the remainder of his family beyond the Mississippi. This purpose as has been intimated, was not executed. Mr. Brown did not proceed to the Arkansas country until more than four years after this time, and not till the beloved daughter, for whose society he was so desirous, had been laid in the dust. The causes of this delay are unknown to the author of this memoir.

Catharine ascribed the change in the intentions of her parents respecting her, wholly to the special providence of Him, who heareth prayer. The appointed time for their departure drew near. She was convinced that it was not best for her to go. Her continual intercessions were, that her parents might be induced to leave her behind. And her prayers were answered. After one of her seasons of private devotion, she returned to her family, with a delightful confident hope, that God had listened to her requests; and as she entered the room where her parents were sitting, she found they had been consulting on the expediency of sending her back to Brainerd; and had actually resolved upon her return. This was just half a year from the period of her removal from that consecrated place.

On this occasion the missionaries very naturally exclaim;--"How unsearchable are the ways of God! We thought it a very afflicting providence that this lamb should be snatched from the fold of Christ, to go, as we thought, where she would be exposed to be devoured by wolves; and were ready to say in our hearts, when her father required her to go with him, 'not so.' But in this very way, God has given her an opportunity to set an example of filial obedience, by submitting to the authority of a father, in a most painful requisition, and of manifesting her love to the Savior, in her willingness to forsake all for him; and at the same time, has granted her the object of her pious and fervent desire."

With how much delight she revisited the scenes of her first aspirations after God and heaven, will appear in a letter which was written a few days after her arrival at Brainerd.

TO MR. AND MRS. HALL, AT KNOXVILLE.
Brainerd, May 30, 1819.
My dear Brother and Sister,

With pleasure I spend a few moments in writing to you this evening, to tell you of my safe arrival on the 23rd of this month. O how great was the joy that I felt, when meeting the dear family at

Brainerd, with whom I have long desired to be. Yes, dear brother and sister, God has returned me back once more, where I can be with Christian friends, and get more instruction. If it is the Lord's will, I hope to stay here two years longer. O that I might improve the great privileges, which I now enjoy.

It appears strange to me, that I am not more interested in the cause of Christ, when he has done so much for me. But I will now give myself up entirely to Him. I should be willing to leave everything for God, and to undergo any sufferings, if it would but make me humble, and would be for his glory.

My heart bleeds for my people, who are on the brink of destruction. OI pray for me, my dear brother and sister. I long to see you and your little one. I am your affectionate sister.

CATHARINE BROWN.

In November, 1819, we find David Brown, the brother of Catharine, a member of the school, and employed, in connection with another young Indian named John Arch, to assist the Rev. D. S. Butrick, one of the missionaries, at Brainerd, in preparing a Cherokee spelling-book, which was afterwards printed for the use of the schools. We may safely conclude that she, who prayed so earnestly for this brother, when he was absent, would not fail to exert herself for his spiritual good when present. Her efforts, in conjunction with those of the missionaries, were not ineffectual. David became thoughtful—deeply impressed—convinced of his sinfulness and his need of salvation by Jesus Christ—and, early in the year 1820, hopes were entertained, that he had become truly pious.

Soon after this, hearing that their father was ill, these young converts from heathenism went home to see him. They remained at home about seven weeks.

Catharine says, "David seized his Bible as soon as he reached home, and began to read and interpret to his father and mother, and the other members of the family, exhorting them to attend to it as the word of God, to repent of their sins, which he told them were many and great, and to become the followers of the Lord Jesus Christ."

With the father's consent, David maintained the worship of God in the family, morning and evening, and craved a blessing and gave thanks at the table. He also conversed freely with friends and neighbors, boldly professing himself a Christian.

The impression made by this visit, in connection with the previous efforts of Catharine, was such, that when Mr. Brown, after recovering from his illness, brought his children back to

Brainerd, he delivered to the missionaries the following letter, signed by himself and others, headmen and chiefs.

"We, the headmen, chiefs of the Creek-Path town, Cherokee nation, have this day assembled ourselves together for the purpose of devising some plan for the education of our children. We daily witness the good effects arising from education, and therefore are extremely anxious to have a school in our neighborhood, as the distance from this part of the nation to Chickamaugah is so great as not to suit our convenience. We therefore solicit your aid in carrying our plan into execution. We can raise twenty, or perhaps twenty-five children. You will please write us immediately on the receipt of this. Given under our hands, this 16th of February, 1820."*

In consequence of this request, Mr. Butrick, who had acquired some knowledge of the Cherokee language, left Brainerd for Creek-Path, on the 11th of March, and, at a place about two miles from Mr. Brown's residence, the natives having erected a convenient house for the purpose, he soon after opened a school, under very favorable auspices.

Mr. Butrick was accompanied and much

---

*This letter, and another from the same quarter on a subsequent page, were thus composed in English, by the help of some white man.

Assisted by John Arch, a converted Cherokee of good promise, whose name has already been mentioned.

This young man was born and bred among the mountains, near the confines of South Carolina, in the most ignorant part of the nation. Happening to be at Knoxville, Tenn. In December, 1818, he saw Mr. Hall, who informed him of the school at Chickamaugah. Returning home, he took his gun, and set off in search of the place. After travelling a hundred and fifty miles, he arrived at the station, told the missionaries he had come to attend the school, and offered them his gun, which was his only property, for clothes. — We are informed his appearance was so wild and forbidding, that the Missionaries hesitated to receive him, especially as he was supposed to be not less than twenty years of age. But he would not be refused. They took him upon trial. It was not long before he discovered an anxious solicitude respecting his soul, and soon gave the most satisfactory evidence of piety. His thirst for knowledge was ardent, and his application and proficiency in learning were gratifying. In ten months he could read and write well. Sometime after he became serious, he was falsely accused, by some one of his school mates, of doing an improper act. Conscious of innocence, he could not well brook the charge. That evening and night he was missing, and the next morning it was concluded that he had absconded. But in the course of the forenoon he made his appearance. On being questioned respecting his absence, he made this reply: "I felt angry, and knew that it was wicked. But I could not suppress it. I therefore went to seek the Savior, that he might reconcile my heart." It appeared, that he had spent the night in devotional exercises. He was at length admitted to the church, and, form that day to the present, has sustained a good Christian character. He has been much employed as an interpreter, both at the different stations, and in the evangelical labors of the missionaries in various parts of the nation.

While Mr. Butrick was prosecuting his incipient labors at Cree-Path, Catharine and David were employing themselves diligently at Brainerd. Once, in particular, it is recorded, that, after a prayer meeting conducted by the missionaries, these two young Cherokees, aided by a pious Indian woman of great age, collected a little group of their people, who had come to spend the Sabbath there, and held a religious conference, with prayer and praise, all in the Cherokee language.

These united labors were, however, interrupted, on the 11th of May, never to be resumed, by the departure of David for the Foreign Mission School in Cornwall, Connecticut.

He left Brainerd only a few days after his admission to the church.

David had been desirous, for some time, of being fitted to preach the Gospel to his countrymen, and was encouraged to aim at such a preparation, first by his sister Catharine, and then by the missionaries. He arrived at Cornwall, sometime in the summer; was connected with that highly favored school about two years; was the removed to Andover, Mass. Where he remained a year, and, without becoming a member of the Theological Institution in that place, enjoyed many of its distinguished advantages. In consequence of the state of his health, and of the great need of his services among those of his countrymen, who reside in the Arkansas country, he returned to them, early in the year 1824. The addresses, which he delivered in many of our principal towns and cities, on the wrongs and claims and prospects of the American Indians, will not soon be forgotten by those who listened to them.

Since his return, a letter has been received, by the Corresponding Secretary of the American Board, which, coming from one so nearly related to Catharine, and giving an amiable view of her family, will interest the reader. It was dated "Point Pleasant, Arkansas, September 20, 1824," and is as follows:

Dear Sir,

Long before this time, you must have head of my speedy passage from Washington City to Arkansas, and of my delightful and joyful meeting with my brethren and kindred according to the flesh. My father and mother embraced me with tears. We were unable to converse, for more than an hour: our mutual joy was so great, that we could not speak for some time. My friends ran as far as they could see me, in order to meet me, and embrace me. The scene was somewhat similar to Jacob meeting with his beloved son Joseph.

I was glad to find so much religious feeling among my friends. My parents are very useful in this country, by making known to others the way of salvation. Since my arrival I have had no rest. My friends and relatives are so numerous, that I am constantly on a visit. Dwight, and the residence of my brother Webber, I have made my homes. At Dwight I have all my books. On the Sabbath, I interpret English sermons, and sometimes preach myself in the sweet language of *Tsallakee*, [the Cherokee.] Never were there greater prospects of success among the Cherokees, than at present.

I expect to revisit my mother-country soon, on my father's business and once more to be at Brainerd and Creek-Path, beneath the tall trees of *Tsu-saw-ya wa sha*. In November and December please write me at Brainerd, and inform me whether the Board can send us a printer, who is accomplished in his art. Pray send us one.

My fond remembrance of your family. Time and distance can never erase from my bosom the marks of friendship and attention I received in Boston. DAVID BORWN.

About the time of David's departure from New England, Mr. Butrick's school at Creek-Path, had so increased in the number of its scholars, that there was no more room for the admission of other applicants. The people therefore desired another school. They said, if a female would come to instruct their daughters, they would build a school-house for her. At the same time, it was evident, that a spirit of deep seriousness and anxious inquiry was beginning to prevail among them.

These facts being known at Brainerd, the missionaries thought it their duty to advise Catharine to go and take charge of the contemplated school. In this advice she acquiesced, though not without a painful diffidence of her qualifications for such a service.

When it was known at Creek-Path, that she was to take charge of the school, the most enthusiastic joy was occasioned among the people.—They seemed to feel, that the preparations could not be made too soon. Not less than fifty Cherokee men, besides negroes and boys, assembled immediately to build a house, which in two days, was nearly completed according to their stipulation.

Everything being in readiness, Mr. Brown came for his daughter. She was a Taloney, the missionary station where her friends Mr. and Mrs. Hall resided, and he waited at Brainerd for her return; during which time it was perceived, that the venerable old man was anxiously inquiring after the truth. On the last of May, 1820, a little less than two years and eleven months from her first entering the school, as an untaught heathen girl, Catharine bade an affectionate adieu to Brainerd, to take charge of the school for females near her parental home. The following entry was made at this time:

"31. Catharine left us, in company with her father, to go to Creek-Path, to teach a school of females.

"How very different the scene from that, which passed here not quite two years since, when her father required her to leave the society of Christians, and to accompany him to the then dark shades of the Arkansas! Now, he does not ask her without our consent; will not take her except by our advice; and she is going, not into the wilderness unprepared to teach, but into a place where divine light has already begun to spring up, prepared as we think, to instruct others. Yet, it is highly probable, that this removal will not be productive of so much good as the former. So unsearchable are the ways of God, and so incompetent is man to judge. It now appears that her first removal was the means of sowing the seed, which is not springing up at Creek-Path with such hopeful promise."

The letters written during the period embraced by this chapter, will, now be inserted. The fourth was originally published at the close of the narrative of the "Little Osage Captive."

TO MR. AND MRS. WILLIAMS.
Brainerd, July 5, 1819.
My dear Brother and Sister Williams,

Although I have long omitted answering your affectionate letters, my heart has been often with you. Yes, dear brother and sister, I do not forget you, and all the pleasant meetings we had together, when you were here. But pain is mixed with pleasure, when I think they are gone no more to return! When I remember the kind instruction I received from you, before you left this place, my heart swells with gratitude. I feel much indebted to you, but more particularly to that God, who sent you here to instruct the poor ignorant Indians in the way that leads to everlasting life. Oh, my dear friends, may the Lord ever bless you, and make you the instrument of doing great good where he has called you.

You may pass through many trials; but remember, beloved brother and sister, all our trials here will only make us richer there when we arrive at our home. A few more days, and then I hope our weary souls will be at rest in our Savior's kingdom, where we shall enjoy His blessed presence forever.

When I wrote you before I expected to go to the Arkansas, and never see this place again. But the Lord has in mercy ordered it otherwise. He has permitted me to live with the dear missionaries here again, though my parents could not bear to think of leaving me behind. My mother said, If I remained here, she did not expect to see me again in this world. Indeed she wished she had never sent me to this school, and that I had never received religious instruction. I told her if she was a Christian, she would not feel so. She would be willing to give me, and all she had, up to Christ. I told her I did not wish to stay on account of my own pleasures; but that I wished to get more instruction, so that it might be for her good, as well as for mine.

I felt very sorry for my poor parents. I thought it was my duty to go in obedience to their commands, and commit myself to the will of God.

I knew the Lord could change the hearts of my parents.

They are now perfectly willing that I should stay here two years longer. I left them in March. They expected to set out in that month for the Arkansas. They had already prepared for the journey. But the Lord has so ordered, that they have concluded not to go until next fall. I don't know whether they will go then. I hope you will pray for them, and also for me, that I may be useful to my dear people. My heart bleeds for their immortal souls. O that I might be made the means of turning many souls from darkness unto marvelous light.

My dear brother and sister, I love you much, and feel that the time is short when we shall sit down with our Savior, and experience that love which no words can describe.

Give my love to my dear brother and sister Kingsbury, and also to all the dear missionaries there. From your affectionate sister in Christ,

CATHARINE BROWN.

P. S. Please to accept this small present for my little darlings, and learn them to say, 'Aunt Catharine.'*

---

*Any person who had witnessed the separation of Mrs. Williams from her Cherokee friends, when she and her husband left Brainerd, and set out for the Choctaw mission, in May, 1818, could well understand the affectionate expressions in this letter.

When the board was ready to proceed, and the hour of parting had arrived; when Mr. Cornelius made the last prayer, and the last hymn had been sung; Catharine was among those who seemed ready to sink under a burden of grief to great to be borne. Mrs. Williams had always been peculiarly dear to her from their first acquaintance, and like an older sister, had guided her youthful steps in the paths of peace.

TO MR. MOODY HALL, AT TALONEY*
Brainerd, Oct. 25, 1819

A few moments of this day shall be spent in writing to my dear brother. It seems a long time since you left us. I long to see you. I long to hear from you. I hope the Lord is with you this day, that you enjoy the presence of our dear Redeemer. My sincere desire and earnest prayer to the throne of grace, is, that your labors may be blessed, and that God would make you the instrument of saving many souls from eternal destruction.

O how I feel for my poor Cherokee brethren and sisters, who do not know the blessed Jesus, that died for us, and do not enjoy the blessings that I do. How thankful I ought to be to God, that I have ever been brought to the light of the Gospel, and was not left to wander in darkness. O I hope the time is a hand, when all the heathen shall know God, whom to know is life everlasting.

My deal brother, may we be faithful to our

---
*Now called Carmel.

Master, knowing that in due season we shall reap, if we faint not. Our pilgrimage will shortly be ended, and all our trials will be over. Do not forget me in your daily prayers, for I need very much the prayers of God's children. My heart is prone to leave my God, whom I love. From your unworthy sister in Christ.

CATHARINE BROWN.

TO MR. AND MRS. HALL,
On their removal from Brainerd,

Brainerd, Nov.--, 1819.

How solemn, my dear brother and sister, is the idea, that we must soon part. Perhaps the next time we meet will be in eternity, before the bar of God. O my dear brother and sister, if we are prepared to meet our God in peace, we shall surely be happy. But, my beloved friends, how can I be permitted to meet you in heaven! My heart is so prone to sin against God, that I am sometimes afraid he will leave me. Forget not to pray, that all these doubts may be removed from me, and that my soul may be washed in the blood of Jesus Christ.

I love you much, and feel that the time is short when we shall sit down with our Savior. Farewell, my dear brother and sister. May the Lord go with you. From your sister.

Catharine.

TO A LADY IN CONNECTICUT.

Brainerd, June 12, 1820.

Dear sister in Christ,

    I thank you much for your affectionate letter, which I received on the 23d of December. O, how great, how rich is the mercy of our dear Redeemer, who has made us the subjects of his kingdom, and led us, as we trust from death unto life. My dear sister, I can never express my gratitude to God, for his goodness towards me, and my dear people. Surely it is of his *own glorious mercy,* that he is sending to us the Gospel of the Lord Jesus, in this distant land, where the people had long sat in darkness, and were perishing for lack of the knowledge of God. Blessed be his holy name! O my sister let us rejoice continually in our Lord and Savior, and as we have put on Christ, not only by outward profession, but by inward and spiritual union, let us walk worthy of our high and holy vocation, and show the world that there is something in true religion. And may the Lord give us strength to do his will, and to follow continually the example of our meek and lowly Jesus. I thank you for the present you sent me, which I received as a token of love. The mission family are all well, and also the dear children. Many of them are serious, and we hope they love and pray to God daily. O that I were more engaged for God, to promote his cause, among these dear children, and my people. I am going soon to visit my parents, which is an hundred miles from here, and expect to stay two months. I hope you will pray for me, that the Lord would bless my visit, and renew the hearts of my dear parents.

You sincere friend and sister in Christ,
CATHARINE BROWN

TO MRS. ISABELLA HALL, AT TALONEY.
Brainerd, March 8, 1820

My dear Sister,

It is with pleasure I take time this morning to assure you, that my love for you is still as great as ever. You cannot tell how painful it was to me to hear that you had been sick. But we know that the Lord is good, and that all things will work together for good to those who love him, and put their trust in him. O could we see each other, how would we talk, and weep, and sing, and pray together.

But our Heavenly Father has separated us. Perhaps we loved each other more than we loved him, and did not pray to him, and praise him, and thank him, as we ought to have done. And is it not so, dear sister? Did we not neglect our duty, and grow cold and careless, when we were together? Now we are sorry, and the Lord will forgive us. Still, dear sister, we can pray for each other. Think you not that our prayers often meet at the throne of grace? O then let us pray on, and never cease to pray for each other, while he lends us breath; and when we meet in heaven, we shall see him whom our soul loveth.

Let us praise the Lord for what he is doing. My dear brother David is now rejoicing in his blessed Redeemer. He has a great desire to do good among our people. I expect he will leave us, in two or three weeks, for Cornwall, to study divinity, and prepare to preach the Gospel of Jesus Christ. I do hope and pray that the Lord will go with him, and enable him to do much good in the world.

He an myself spent seven weeks with our dear parents, and returned to school the last week. I hope to continue here some time longer, but know not how long. My dear mother feels that she cannot spare me much longer, I wish to learn as much as I can, before I go.

And now, my dear sister, may we both be faithful to our Lord, and do much in the world. And when time with us shall be no more, may we be permitted to meet in that world, where Christians will be collected to sing through eternity the son of Moses and the Lamb.

From your sister
CATHARINE BROWN.

TO HER BROTHER DAVID,
While on his way to New England.

Brainerd, May 16, 1820.

My very Dear Brother,

I cannot express my feelings this evening, when I read your kind letter. My heart is full. But we know, dear brother, that our Savior orders all things right. I am very sorry to hear that you have lost your horse. What will you do now? But let us not be troubled about these things. If it is best that you should go on, the Savior will provide for you in some way. Let us only, my dear brother, put our whole trust in God, and be humble at the feet of Jesus. We can do nothing of ourselves. We are like little children. If we rely on our own strength, we shall fall. It is impossible for me to express what I felt, the morning you left us. But I thought, that if I should never see you again in this world, I should meet you in a better, where there will be no separation. O how thankful we ought to be to God, who has brought us from darkness into the light of the Gospel.

But many of our dear people are yet deprived of this great privilege. They know not the Savior, whom we have found so precious. Yes, even our dear parents are yet living without any hope in God. O my brother, let us never cease to pray for them. God will surely hear us, if we ask in faith.

Dear brother, forget me not in your prayers.

You sister C. will never forget you. When you are far from this place, your poor sister C. will be praying for you. God night, dear brother, till we meet again.

                                        CATHARINE BROWN

CHAPTER 4.
FROM HER TAKING CHARGE OF A SCHOOL AT CREEK-PATH, UNTIL HER SICKNESS

We now enter upon the last three, and the most interesting years of Catharine's life, in which we shall behold her in new circumstances; her character more fully developed; and her graces shining with greater luster.

In order that she may speak for herself as much as possible, that part of her private diary will be inserted, which was saved from the destruction, to which many of her papers were devoted, a little before her sickness. It was obtained from Mrs. Gilbreth, a sister of Catharine, and a faithful copy was transmitted by Mrs. Potter, the wife of the Rev. William Potter, missionary at Creek-Path. It commences the day before her departure from Brainerd.

EXTRACTS FROM HER DIARY.

"Brainerd, May 20, 1820. Tomorrow morning I shall leave this school, perhaps never to return. It is truly painful to part with my dear Christian friends, those with whom I have spent many happy hours in the house of worship. I must bid them farewell. This is the place, where I first became acquainted with the dear Savior. He now calls me to work in his vineyard, and shall I, for the sake of my Christian friends and of my own pleasures, refuse to go, while many of my poor red brothers and sisters are perishing for lack of knowledge? O no. I *will not* refuse to go. I will go wherever the Savior calls me. I know he will be on my right hand, to grant me all the blessings, that I shall need, and he will direct me how to instruct the dear children, who shall be committed to my care.

"This morning I set out from Brainerd, with my dear father. Travelled about twenty miles. Thought much of my beloved Christian friends. Whether I shall ever see them again, is uncertain. The Lord only knows.

"June 2. Have been very sick today; but blessed be God, am now a little better. Hope I shall be able to travel tomorrow. The Lord is very kind and merciful to all those, who put their trust in him. Last night I slept on the floor without any bed. Felt quite happy in my situation. Though very sick in body, yet I trust my heart was well.

"5. Have arrived at my father's but am yet very unwell. Have a bad cold. Am sometimes afraid I shall not be able to teach school at Creek Path. We slept two nights on the ground with our wet blankets, before we reached our home.

"20. Blessed be God, who has again restored me to health. It is two weeks today since I commenced teaching a girls school. O how much I need wisdom from God. I am a child. I can do nothing. But in God will I trust, for I know there is none else, to whom I can look for help.

"Sept. 5. This day I received a letter from brother David. I rejoice much to hear, that he has arrived safely at Cornwall. May the Lord be with him, and make him useful as long as he lives, and at death may he be received at the right hand of God. This the prayer of his affectionate sister Catharine."

Before proceeding further with the extracts from the diary, it seems proper to insert some notices not found in that document.

Catharine opened her school with about twenty scholars, and the number soon increased. Not only the daughters but the mothers also, manifested a strong desire to receive instruction. Several of her pupils, in consequence of previous tuition, could read in the New Testament, when they came under her care. These it was her delight to lead to a more perfect acquaintance with that sacred volume. But most of the children began with the rudiments of learning. This school she continued three quarters of a year, much to the satisfaction of her scholars, their parents, and the missionaries. She finally relinquished it, only because the arrival of Mr. and Mrs. Potter gave her an opportunity to surrender her charge into other hand, and at the same time opened the way for her prosecuting higher studies, with a view to greater usefulness to her people.

The spirit of serious inquiry at Creek Path, to which an allusion has already been made, increased after the arrival of Catherine, especially among her own kindred. Doubtless she was not backward, with the meekness of humility and with the earnestness of affection, to warn and exhort. Nor were her efforts without effect. Ere long she had the joy of beholding her father, mother, a brother, and two or three sisters, unitedly seeking the pardon of their sins, and that peace, which the world giveth not. After a suitable trial, and due instruction, all these her relatives, with others of their countrymen, publicly professed faith in Christ, and were unite to his visible church.

It is gratifying to be able to remark, that no one of them has hitherto dishonored the Christian profession, and that all who survive, are believed to be the humble followers of the Lord Jesus. One has "fallen asleep," and of him an affectionate record will be found in that part of Catharine's diary which is yet to be inserted.

Sometime in the autumn, nearly the whole family made a visit to Brainerd. The hearts of the missionaries were made glad, by the sight of this little band: And oh! How must the heart of Catharine have exulted with joy, while, for the first time, she presented her beloved relatives, one after another, as the friends and followers of her blessed Savior!

It will be remembered that a letter from the chiefs at Creek Path, desiring the missionaries to establish a school among them, was inserted in the last chapter. Mr. Brown was now the bearer of another letter from the same chiefs, signed by their Chairman, or Speaker, in which they thus express their approbation of the school and their good wishes with respect to missionary efforts.

"Friends and Brothers,

"We are glad to inform you, that we are well pleased with Mr. Butrick, who has come forward as a teacher to instruct our people. We believe he does discharge his duty; and we hope his coming will be of great advantage to our people. Our wish is, that you may prosper throughout our nation, in your laudable undertaking. It is out of our power to see you, in any short time, on account of the National Council, and other business we are obliged to attend at this time. It is our wish that the school should continue at this place. Mr. John Brown, Sr. will deliver this, who will present you our hands in friendship. We hope we shall see each other before long. We are glad to see our children advancing so well. We conclude with our best respects.

WAU-SAU-SEY, *Bear-meat*, Speaker."

Here some remarks may properly be introduced, on the traits of character, which Catharine exhibited, during a part of the time embraced in her diary. These remarks are taken from the letter of Mrs. Potter, which enclosed that document.

"In the spring of 1821, while making the necessary preparations for a settlement at Creek-Path, Mr. Potter and myself for two months, made Mr. Brown's house our home. Here we had an opportunity of noticing Catharine's daily deportment, as a member of the domestic circle.

"For sweetness of temper, meekness, gentleness, and forbearance, I never saw one, who surpassed her. To her parents she was uncommonly dutiful and affectionate. Nothing which could contribute to their happiness, was considered a burden; and her plans were readily yielded to theirs, however great the sacrifice to her feelings. The spiritual interest of the family lay near her heart, and she sometimes spent whole evenings in conversation with them on religious subjects.

"Nor did she forget the poor slaves. Having, at her own expense, put a spelling book into the hands of each of the younger ones, she began with zeal to teach them to read. One of these she had the happiness, before her death, of seeing able to read the New Testament with fluency, committing hymns to memory, etc., and another considerably advanced in the same path.

"She never spoke of any good thing, which she had herself performed, except when circumstances made it her duty, and then it was with great apparent humility.

"Before our arrival, she had established a weekly prayer meeting with the female members of the family, which was also improved as an opportunity for reading the word of God, and conversing upon its important truths. Such was her extreme modesty, that she did not make this known to me, until more than a week after my arrival; and the usual period was passed without a meeting. She at length overcame her diffidence, and in a manner expressive of the most unfeigned humility, informed me what their practice had been. These meetings were continued while we remained in the family, and I believe they were highly useful. A monthly prayer meeting among the sisters of the church was soon after established, in which Catharine took a lively interest; nor did she ever refuse when requested, to take an active part in the devotional exercises.

"Soon after we removed to our station, Catharine became a member of our family, and of the school. All her energies were now bent towards the improvement of her mind, with a view to future usefulness among her people. Both in school, and in the family, her deportment was such as greatly to endear her to our hearts, and she was most tenderly loved by all the children.

"She was not *entirely* free from the inadvertencies of youth; but always received reproof with great meekness, and it never failed to produce the most salutary effect.

"She was deeply sensible of the many favors she had received from Christian friends, and often, in the strongest terms, expressed her gratitude.

"She was zealous in the cause of Christ, and labored much to instruct her ignorant people in the things that concern their everlasting peace. The advancement of the Redeemer's kingdom was to her a subject of deep interest, and she read accounts of the triumphs of the cross in heathen countries, with peculiar delight. Not many months after we settled here, a plan was devised to form a female charitable society. — This plan was proposed to Catharine. She was much pleased with it, and spared no pains to explain it to the understanding of her Cherokee friends. And so successful were her exertions, that, and the meeting for the formation of the Society, at which a considerable number were present, not on refused to become a member. For the prosperity of the Society she manifested the most tender concern till her death; and she had determined, if her life should be spared to reach the Arkansas country, to use her exertions to form a similar Society there."*

The extracts from the diary will now be resumed, and will be continued without interruption.

EXTRACTS FROM HER DIARY.

"Creek-Path, May 1, 1821. Commenced boarding with Mr. and Mrs. Potter. My Parents Live two miles from this place. I think I shall

---

*This Society first sent its annual collections to the mission at Dwight, in the Arkansas. But the last year their collections was devoted to the spread of the Gospel among the Osages. The Cherokee women, who proposed the resolution to appropriate the money in this way, observed to the Society, "The Bible tells us to do good to our enemies, and I believe the Osages are the greatest enemies the Cherokees have." The sum was about ten dollars.

visit them almost every week, and they will come to see me often.

" 2. I love to live here much. It is retired, and a good place for study. Everything looks pleasant around the school-house. The trees are covered with green leaves, and the birds sing very sweetly. How pleasant it is to be in the woods, and hear the birds praising the Lord. — They remind me of the divine command, 'Remember thy Creator,' O may I never be so stupid and senseless [as to forget my Creator,] but may I remember to love and serve him, the few days I live in this world; for the time will soon come, when I must appear before him. Help me, Lord, to live to thy glory, even unto the end of my life.

"I think I feel more anxious to learn, and to understand the Bible perfectly than I ever did before. Although I am so ignorant, the Savior is able to prepare me for usefulness among my people.

" 5. Saturday evening. Again I am brought to the close of another week. How have I spent my time the past week? Have I done anything for god, and any good to my fellow creatures? I fear I have done nothing to glorify his holy name. Oh, how prone I am to sin, and to grieve the Spirit of a holy God, who is so kind in giving me time to prepare for Heaven. May I improve these precious moments to the glory of my God.

" 6. Sabbath evening. How thankful I ought to be to God, that he has permitted me once more to commemorate the love of a Savior, who has shed his precious blood for the remission of sin. It was indeed a solemn season to me, and I hope refreshing to each of our souls. While sitting at the table, I thought of many sins which I had committed against God, through my life, and how much I deserved to be cast out from his presence forever. But the Son of God, who was pleased to come down from the bosom of his Father, to die on the cross for sinners like me, will I hope, save me from death, and at last raise me to mansions of eternal rest, where I shall sit down with my blessed Jesus.

" 8. This evening I have nothing to complain of, but my unfaithfulness both to God and my own soul. Have not improved my precious moments as I ought. Have learned but little in school, though my privileges are greater than those of many others. While they are ignorant of God, and have no opportunity to hear or learn about him, I am permitted to live with the children of God, where I am instructed to read the bible, and to understand the character of Jesus. O may I be enabled to follow the example of my teachers, to live near the Savior, and to do much good. I wish very much to be a missionary among my people. If I had an education—but perhaps I ought not to think of it. I am not worthy to be a missionary.

"14. Mr. Hoyt called on us this week, on his return from Mayhew. He gives us much interesting intelligence respecting the Choctaw mission. My Hoyt expected to have brought Dr. Worcester with him, but he was too sick to travel, and was obliged to stay behind. He hopes to be able to come soon. I long to see him. He has done a great deal towards spreading the Gospel, not only in this nation, but in other heathen nations of the earth. May the Lord restore his health, that he may see some fruits among the heathen, for whom he has been so long laboring.

"29. This day I spent my time very pleasantly at home, with my dear friends. Find that brother John is the same humble believer in Jesus, walking in the Christian path. I am truly happy to meet my ear parents and sisters in health, and rejoicing in the hope of eternal glory. O may God ever delight to bless them, and to pour his spirit richly into their hearts. I am much pleased to see them making preparations for the Sabbath. They have been engaged today in preparing such food, etc., as they thought would be wanting tomorrow. I think brother John, and sister Susannah have done much good here, with respect to the Sabbath.

"30. This day attended another solemn meeting in the house of God. Mr. Potter preached by an interpreter. I think more people than usual attended. All seemed attentive to hear the word of God. Mr. P. spoke of the importance of keep8ing the Sabbath holy. I hope it will not be in vain to all those who were present.

"June 4. This day being the *first Monday in the month,* the people met to pray, and receive religious instruction. It was truly an interesting time. The congregation, though small, was serious. One man and his wife, who have been for some time in an anxious state of mind, remained after the meeting, and Mr. and Mrs. P. earnestly entreated them to seek the Lord while he was near unto them. They appeared very solemn, and said they wished to know more about God, that they might serve him the rest of their days. We hope and pray, that they may be truly converted, and become our dear brother and sister in the Lord.

"July 1. This day I have enjoyed much.—Was permitted once more to sit down at the table of the Lord, and commemorate his dying love. O how good is the Savior in permitting me to partake of his grace. May I improve my great privileges in the manner I shall wish I had done, when I come to leave the world.—P.M. Went to Mr. G's where Mr. Potter preaches once in two weeks. Most of the people present were whites, from the other side of the river. It was pleasant to hear a sermon preached without an interpreter.

"Sept. 2. Think I have had a good time today, in praying to my heavenly father. I see nothing to trouble me, but my own wicked heart. It appears to me, that the more I wished to serve God, the more I sin. I seem never to have done anything good in the sight of God. But the time is short, when I shall be delivered from this body of sin, and enter the kingdom of heaven.

"3. The first Monday in the Month. No doubt many Christians have been this day praying for my poor nation, as well as for other heathen nations of the earth. O why do I live so little concerned for my own soul, and for the souls of others? Why is it that I pray no more to God? Is it because he is not merciful? Oh no. He is good, kind, merciful, always ready to answer the prayers of his children. O for more love to my Savior than I now have.

" 4. I am now with my sister, with whom I expect to spend a few days. I hope the Lord will make our communion sweet.

"Visited at Mr.—'s; but had no opportunity of conversing with Mrs.— on religious subjects, as we intended to have done. Mr.— said he had seen so many different ways among professed Christians, that it was hard to tell who was right. I felt too ignorant to instruct such a well educated man; though I knew, that there is *but one* way under heaven, whereby men can be saved, and that is, by coming to him, who came to seek and to save, that which was lost.

" 9. Returned yesterday from sister G's.—Found the mission family in good health; I cannot express how much I love the missionaries, with whom I life. I do not feel my privileges, until I am away from them, and mingle with worldly people. Then I long to get back to be with Christians.

"I rejoice and bless my heavenly Father, that he has kept my dear brother John, and permitted me to meet him once more in the land of the living. I am sorry to see him so unwell, and fear he will not recover. But the Lord's will be done, and not mine. I know that he will do all things for the good of those who love him.

"Left home, in company with brother John and sister Susannah, [his wife,] for the purpose of visiting the Sulpher Springs, in Blount county, Alabama.

" 21. About noon, we came to a spring, which is said to posses the same qualities with those we intended to visit, and we concluded to make it the place of our abode for a few days. We therefore, pitched our tent a few yards from the water, and at night spread our blankets on the ground, and slept very well.

" 22. Feel very uneasy respecting my brother,

he is so unwell. May the Lord be with us in this lonely place.

" 23. Brother John drinks the water, and bathes in it, but has yet received no benefit. I do not feel so well as I did before I came here, and almost wish to return immediately. Perhaps it is lying on the ground, that makes me feel sick. But if brother John had a comfortable place to sleep, I should not care for myself.—The Lord knows what is best for us.

" 24. We expect a boy with our horses today, and hope to reach home tomorrow. Saw Mr. J. R. today in a very low state of health. Conversed with him a little on the subject of religion. This I really felt was my duty, as I thought it likely I should never have another opportunity. He said he was very wicked, and afraid to die. I told him we were all wicked, but the Savior, who was willing to die for us would pardon our sins, if we would only give ourselves to him. He replied, that when he was in health, he did not do his duty towards God, but if he recovered, he would try to do better. As he was not able to converse much, I commended him to God, and left him. God is able to make him his dear child, and prepare him for heaven.

" Jan. 3, 1822. This was truly a solemn and interesting day to me, one which will never be forgotten. My dear father and mother were baptized in the name of the Holy Trinity. How kind is our Creator, in his willingness to take notice of us sinful worms of the dust, and allowing us to become acquainted with Jesus Christ. O may we walk close with God, and be enabled to set such an example to others, that they may be led to glorify our Father, who is in heaven.

" 14. Have not attended school since last vacation, having been at home taking care of my sick brother. He has failed very fast, the past week. I fear he will not live many days. The will of the Lord be done.

" 16. My dear brother is very low. Perhaps he will soon depart from this sinful world, and fly to the arms of his blessed Redeemer. Had some conversation with him this evening. His mind seemed to be in a happy state. He asked me, whether after his decease, I thought we should stay here, or go to the Arkansas. I told him I hoped he would be restored to health. He said, he thought that was very doubtful, and added, that he thought brother Webber would come for us after his departure. My heart was full. I could make no reply.

" 18. Mr. Butrick and John Arch, who have been visiting us for a few days past, left us this morning, with the intention of going through the nation, preaching Jesus Christ to those who are in darkness. This will probably take three months. May the Lord go with his dear servants on their long journey through the wilderness, and bless their labors to many immortal souls. I cannot sufficiently express my gratitude to God, for sending out missionaries to this distant land, that we, who were wanders in the wild woods, might find the road to heaven. How kindly are they inviting us to come and partake of the rich feast, which has been provided for all who will accept it. Yet how few are willing to comply with the invitation! Frequently do I weep for my Cherokee brothers and sisters, when I consider their awful situation while out of Christ; and willingly would I offer myself for their assistance, were I qualified for a religious teacher. I hope God will prepare me to do some good among the heathen. O that it may be my greatest desire to do the will of my heavenly Father. I am determined to pray for my people, while God lends me breath; and when I die, may my savior receive me to my heavenly home, to join with millions of saints, in singing the praises of redeeming love through a never-ending eternity.

" 29. Eternity seems near. A few days more, and if I am indeed a child of God, I shall walk the golden streets of the New Jerusalem. O happy day, when I shall see all the Christians, who have ever lived, and when God himself shall be my joy.

" 30. Brother John is senseless most of the time. I fear he is to remain but a little while in this world. But in that case, he will soon go to his Father in heaven. May we be submissive, knowing that he, who sent us into this world has a right to call us hence whenever he sees best. Our great consolation is, that our dear brother will soon be freed from pain, and rest in the bosom of his dear Jesus.

" 31. Had the pleasure of seeing Mr. and Mrs. Potter at this place. I love them as my own brother and sister.

"Feb. 2. My dear brother very sick. O thou blessed Jesus, take him not away by this sickness. Restore him to health, that he may live long, and be a great blessing to our nation. But O may I be submissive to thy holy will.

"Sabbath morning. Painful it is to record, that my dear brother John appears, this day, to be on the borders of eternity! Lord come near to us at this time. Help us to give up our dear brother into thy hands.

"Evening. Brother John is no more! O distressing thought, he has gone to return no more! But we shall soon go to him. I trust, indeed, we have much reason to believe he has gone to Christ his Savior. Through his sickness he seemed reconciled to the will of God, and said he was not afraid to die. He said, that though his sufferings were great, they were nothing in comparison with Christ's sufferings. About a week before he died, he spoke to the family as follows:—"It is now more than a year since we began to follow Christ, and what have we done for him? Do we live like Christians? I fear we do not. I do not hear you talk to the people about our Savior when they come to visit you. We are professors of religion, and why is it that we do not show it to others? You should always remember to keep the Sabbath holy. You are too much occupied in domestic concerns on the Sabbath, so that you cannot get time to converse about God. He asked me, if the missionaries did their cooking on the Sabbath. I told him, their preparations were made before the Sabbath. He said, 'That is what we ought to do.' He frequently requested me to read and explain the Bible to him, which was my great delight."

Here ends her diary. And the reader will doubtless wish that all had been saved, breathing, as it does, so much good sense and unfeigned piety.

Of her brother John, the Journal of the mission at Brainerd contains the following eulogium, penned on hearing of his death.

"Two years ago he was in heathenish darkness. About that time his brother and sister told him of the Bible, and some of the important truths it contained; and he soon felt an unconquerable desire to read it. He could then talk and understand familiar English. Soon after, a school was opened in his neighborhood, and he applied himself, with the most unwearied diligence, to study. In the course of six months, he learned to read intelligibly: read the New Testament through once, and about half through again; wrote a number of legible letters to his friends; became a hopeful convert to the Christian religion, and a member of the church of Christ, which he continued to adorn by an exemplary life, till his departure from these dark and afflictive scenes, to join, as we trust, the Church of the first born in heaven."

Not long after the decease of this brother, Catharine accompanied her father to Huntsville, in the state of Alabama.

Here, either at the time or later in the season, she spent two or three months, in the family of Dr. Alexander A. Campbell, a pious and esteemed physician. Dr. Campbell had seen her at her father's house before she went to Brainerd, and was so favorably impressed, by her personal appearance, that he subsequently procured for her a Bible, and some other religious books, which were forwarded, but never received.

Nearly five years had elapsed since that

interview. Dr. Campbell's own words, extracted from a letter to the Rev. Mr. Potter of Creek-Path, shall describe the impression, which she now made upon him, and upon others in Huntsville.

"She was not now the wild untutored girl she was then. She was graceful and polite, and humility and benevolence beamed from her countenance. Some of my acquaintance were unwilling to believe she was an Indian.

"At your request, I returned with her to her nation to see a diseased Indian child, and though it was at the expense of neglecting important professional business, I was amply repaid, by the interesting conversation I had with her, on literary and religious subjects.

"At first, she was backward to enter into free conversation. A diffident reserve was a prominent trait in her character. But when we became well acquainted, I found her perfectly agreeable and intelligent on any ordinary subject. But her favorite theme was the SAVIOR. She dwelt much, also, on the situation of her people, and manifested the greatest solicitude for their spiritual interests; often expressing the hope, that I would come and live among them, and teach them respecting the Lord Jesus.

"During the summer of this year, she spent several months in my family. A part of that time she was suffering very severely from a bilious fever which she bore with all possible patience and resignation, never showing that peevishness and fretfulness so common in persons from that disease. She always looked upon her afflictions as resulting from the chastising hand of God, and designed for her improvement.

"She received very marked attentions from the visitors at my house, and many of the principal families in the town sought an acquaintance with her, appeared sensible of her worth, and esteemed her friendship highly. These attentions, so far from exciting her vanity, had the effect to humble her the more. She appeared ever to think much less highly of herself than others thought of her. I have often been astonished to see how the flattering addresses and high encomiums of people of elevated standing in society, seemed to render her more distrustful of her own worth."

This, though evidently the warm language of friendship, is justified by the concurrent testimony of all the intimate friends of Catharine.

In September, 1822, at the earnest request of her parents, she left the family of Mr. Potter to reside with them. Being engaged, at that time, in some favorite studies, it was a great trial to leave the school. But so tender was her regard for her aged parents, that she made not the least objection.

Near the close of the year 1822, the Rev.

Reynolds Bascom, accompanied by several Indian youths from the Foreign Mission School at Cornwall, arrived at Creek-Path, on his way to Elliot, where he designed to spend a few months in missionary labor.

"Here," says Mr. Bascom, "I had an opportunity of seeing the precious fruits of missionary instruction and divine grace, in the intelligence, amiable manners, and Christian temper of Catharine, and other members of the little church, which had been formed in the place, chiefly among her family connections.

"The impression made on my mind by my first interview, which was at her father's house, was that of uncommon simplicity, modesty and meekness. We arrived after the family had dined, and she received us and spread a table for our refreshment, with the unaffected kindness of a sister. The gracefulness of her figure, and the sweetness of her expression, have often been the subject of remark; and I was the more delighted with her humility, as I greatly feared I should discover an unhappy influence from the misjudged praise, which had been heaped upon her. The fact was, she gave me evidence by her habitual behavior, of being a sanctified child of God.

It was soon after her removal to her paternal home, that the disease, the seeds of which, had probably for several years, been germinating in her constitution, began to assume an aspect which excited some alarm.

In consequence of this, she took a journey to Brainerd, in February, 1823, with the view of consulting Dr. Butler, a medical gentleman residing at that station. She hope, also to derive benefit from the journey. These hopes were disappointed. A cold, tempestuous storm arose, soon after she left home, to the whole of which she was unavoidably exposed; and the slight cough, to which she had, for some time, been subject, was very much increased. She spent three weeks at Brainerd, and then returned to Creek-Path, intending to obtain permission from her parents to place herself again under the care of Dr. Butler. But her increased illness rendered her unable to encounter the fatigues of another journey.

The narrative must now be interrupted, in order that several letters, written during the time embraced by this chapter, may be introduced. A part of the first, and the fourth, were published in the narrative of the "Little Osage Captive." The third made its first appearance in a religious paper published at New Haven.

TO HER BROTHER DAVID, AT CORNWALL.

Creek-Path, Aug. 12th, 1820.

My dear Brother,

Your dear lines I received this evening, for which I thank you. I hope they will not be the last you will write me. O dear brother, how much it would rejoice my heart to see you this evening and converse with you, face to face! But our good Lord has separated us perhaps never to see each other again in this world. I often think of the morning you left Brainerd. It was a solemn hour, and I trust it was a sweet season to our souls. We wept, and prayed, and sang together, before our dear Savior; and longed for that blessed day, when we should meet to part no more. What is a short separation in this world? Nothing compared to an eternal separation! How thankful we ought to be then, my dear brother, that we have a hope to be saved through the blessed Lamb of God. Yes, I trust when our bodies shall die, our souls shall be raised above the sky, where we shall dwell together, in singing the praises of him who bought us with his precious blood. I hope we shall meet our parents, and brothers and sisters there. Since you left, the Lord has reached down his arm, to take sinners from darkness into the marvelous light of the Gospel. Dear Brother, let us praise and rejoice continually in the Lord, for his goodness to our dear people, in giving them hearts to love and praise his holy name. Surely the Lord is with us here. We feel his presence. Our dear father and mother are inquiring what they shall do to be saved.—Mother says she is grieved to think her children are going to leave her behind. But she says she will pray as long as she lives, and that the Savior will pardon her sins, that she may go with her children to heaven.

I hope you will write to our parents as often as you can. I sometimes think the Savior has given them new hearts, especially our dear father. He appears quite changed.

Soon after you left Brainerd, I was called here to take charge of a school of females, about two miles from home. I take great delight in teaching. The number of girls in school is twenty-eight. They are very good children, and learn fast. Sister Anna is assisting me in the school. She rejoices with us to hear from you in this distant land.

O dear brother, I hope you will pray for me. Pray that I may do good to the immortal souls of my pupils. Sometimes the work appears too great for me, and I am almost discouraged. But I know, He that has called me to work in his vineyard, is able to keep me.

I could tell you a great many good things, if I had time. But I must stop, after asking your prayers for all your Creek-Path friends. I hope when you return to your nation, you will find many Christians. Farewell, dear brother, may the Lord be with you, and prepare you for great usefulness in the world. This is the prayer of your sister,

CATHARINE BROWN.

TO MR. AND MRS. HALL,
Creek-Path, Nov. 19, 1820

My dear Brother and Sister

This is the first opportunity I have had to answer the kind letter, which you wrote some time since. I thank you for it, and hope you will forgive me for not writing sooner. I think of you every day, and long to see you once more in this world. I often think of the happy hours we used to spend together, while I was with you at Brainerd. But the happy hours are gone, I fear never to return. I hope, if we may not meet in this world, we may in heaven, where we shall never be separated. O, my friends do you not sometimes long to see that glorious day, when Christians shall be gathered from all parts of the world to sing the praises of our dear Redeemer? What a day it will be for Christians! And shall we be among the number? Sometimes I fear I shall not be, my wicked heart is so prone to sin. But I know the blood of Christ is sufficient to wash away all my sins, and prepare me for his eternal glory. I will, therefore, commit myself to God. It is all that I can do.

O, how good it is to lie at the feet of Jesus, and feel ourselves purified by his blood. Then we have no reason to fear what the world can do unto us.

My dear friends, I cannot tell you how much I love you, because you were willing to leave your native land, and your dear people, to come into this heathen part of the world, to instruct me and my people in the way of salvation. May the Lord reward you for this labor of love.—Probably you must have some trials to pass through, as other missionaries do; but we ought to rejoice, that we are accounted worthy to labor for God. Our days will soon be past, and if we are the children of God, we shall soon be at rest in the bosom of our dear Savior.

My father, mother, brothers, and sisters, wish to be remembered affectionately to you. Write often. I am always happy to hear from you

From your sister,
CATHARINE BROWN.

TO HER BROTHER DAVID, AT CORNWALL.
Creek-Path, Feb. 21, 1821.
My dear Brother,

I received your kind letter some time since, and it gave me great satisfaction to hear from you. I should have written to you before this time, but did not know how to send to Brainerd. I am truly happy to hear that you feel so well contented with your situation in school, and that you are well pleased with your dear instructor. Our dear parents are in good health. They have removed from the place where they lived before, and are now living with brother John. I think they have truly passed from death unto life. They seem to be growing in grace and in the knowledge of Him, who has redeemed their souls from hell. Indeed, you cannot imagine how different they seem from what they did when you left us. All they desire now, is to do the will of our dear Savior. This work is the Lord's, and no doubt he will carry them safe through this sinful world, until he receives them to his heavenly kingdom. O, dear brother, truly the Lord has heard our prayers for the souls of our parents. We have great reason to rejoice. May we not say,--not unto us, but to thy name be all praise? You have doubtless heard, that brother John has joined the church. Dear brother David, my heart is full while I am writing.—How shall I express my gratitude to God, for bringing him to a knowledge of the Savior. He says sometimes he feels happy in praying to God, and feels wiling that he should do with him as seemeth good in his sight.

My brother David, when we look back and see what the Lord has done for our family in the course of a few years, O let us call upon our souls, and all that is within us, to praise our God for his great blessings to us.

I sometimes long to see your face once more in this world, to converse and pray with you before our Savior. I often think of the happy hours, which we spent when we were at Brainerd, when we first tasted the sweetness of religion, and when we used to take each other's hand to walk and sing our favorite hymn,

"Come we that love the Lord."

We then knew the happiness of saints, and felt that religion was not 'designed to make our pleasures less.' But now our heavenly Father has separated us for a time in this world; I hope for his glory and for the good of perishing souls around us. We have much to do for our Savior. As we hope we are children of the most high God, let us be good soldiers, and not be weary in well-doing, for in due season we shall reap, if we faint not.

Father and mother send love to you, and to the scholars in Cornwall. I hope you will write to us soon, and let us know how you do.

Adieu, dear brother, till we meet again,

CATHARINE BROWN.

TO THE SAME.

Creek-Path, 1821.

My dear Brother,

Although we may be separated many hundreds

of miles, the God of the Universe, whom we serve, will often give us the enjoyment of himself, which you know is of far greater value than all this world can afford. Last Sabbath was a very solemn and interesting day to us. Rev. Mr. W. from the state of New York was here—a very pious and engaged Christian. We were much refreshed by his kind instructions. I think it was truly a pleasant day to my soul. The sacrament was administered, and we were permitted once more to sit at the table of the Lord, and commemorate his dying love. Mr. S. was baptized. Also an infant of Mrs. F. named Samuel Worchester. The congregation were attentive and some of them were affected to tears. I hope the time is not far distant, when all the heathen shall be brought to the knowledge of the Redeemer. We have recently formed a Female Society* in this place. The members pay fifty cents a year. I trust you will pray that we may be blessed, and that we may be instrumental in the great work of building up the cause of the Redeemer. I can never be sufficiently thankful to God for sending us missionaries, to teach us the way we should go. We love them as our own brothers and sisters. That you may enjoy the light

---

*The Society of which mention was made on p. 63.

of our Savior's countenance, while in this short journey of life, and finally be received to mansions of eternal glory, is the prayer of your sister,

CATHARINE BROWN.

TO MR. AND MRS. HALL.

Creek-Path, June 1, 1821.

My dear Brother and Sister Hall,

Sweet and reviving is the thought, that we are not to continue long in this world, but hope soon to rest in the city of our God. My dear brother and sister, be patient in all your trials and hardships, remembering that you are laboring for God, and not for man alone. The Savior will give you an unfading crown of glory in due season. I often think of the glorious day, when I shall meet you, and all good missionaries, in the kingdom of our Savior. I shall then be always with those dear friends, who have told me so much about heaven, and taught me to love and serve Christ. I hope you will not forget to pray, that I may possess more of the spirit of Christ.

The pupils in the school here, generally make good improvement. The religious prospects are encouraging. The meetings on the Sabbath, and weekly conferences, are well attended. The church appears well. Last Sabbath I, for the first time, met my parents at the table of the Lord.

I have many things to tell you; but my health will not allow me to write much at one time.— The he little I have written gives me pain. My health has been feeble for some weeks past, but my complaints are not alarming. I shall try to visit you next vacation, if life is spared. Will my dear brother and sister write soon to their affectionate   CATHARINE.

TO HER BROTHER DAIVD,
Huntsville, Aug. 30, 1822.

My dear brother,

I am sorry to tell you, that I have but a few moments of time to write this evening. I came here the 13th inst. and expect to return in a few weeks.

I left our friends all very well, and walking in the fear of God. I should have written long before this, had I not been sick; but my health is now much better than it was when I left home. Brother David, remember that your sister Catharine loves you much, and prays for you every day. I trust you will not return before you are prepared to preach the Gospel. Let me know your feelings in this respect when you write again, and I shall know how to pray for you. I do not expect you to go through all the studies, that ministers generally do in New England, but wish you to be qualified enough to withstand the enemies of God, and teach the truths of Christianity. If your health does not permit you to study, and your hesitation of speech still continues, I should not think it was your duty to pursue your studies.

However, I know the Lord will make every path of duty plain before you. Do not think we are unhappy. It is true, we were greatly tried last winter, in losing our dear brother. But, blessed be God, it was not more than we are able to bear.

We feel it was good for us to be afflicted, knowing that the Lord is good, and will always do what is right. I have no time to write all I wish to send you. When I return home, you shall have a long letter from your affectionate sister

CATHARINE

TO THE SAME, AT ANDOVER.

Creek-Path, January 18, 1823.

My dear Brother,

Yours of Nov. 2, 1822, was received a few days since. I am much gratified to hear, that you are to continue in New England another year. I hope you will be the better qualified for usefulness to our countrymen, when you return. I pray for you daily, that God may be with you, and bless you in your undertaking.

I feel anxious to see you, yet I am willing to have you stay until you have received further education. How has your mind been exercised since you entered the interesting Seminary at Andover? Are you living in the enjoyment of the religion of Christ? We must, dear brother, live near to God, and be engaged in his cause, if we would be his followers. Let us, then, not calculate to live in idleness and ease unconcerned for the salvation of souls.

We are under great obligations to honor God before the world, and to be active in his service. Let us not hide our talents in the earth, for the Lord will require them of us. There is a crown of glory laid up for those who are faithful unto the end.

It is now eleven months, since our dear brother John departed from this lower world, and entered the unseen regions of eternity, where I hope he is now walking the streets of the New Jerusalem, filled with holy love. Oh boundless love, and matchless grace, of our Lord and Savior Jesus Christ! How happy shall we feel when we land on the shores of eternal felicity.—There we shall meet our dear brother, and all who have gone before us, and shall reign in the paradise of God forever and ever.

I often think of our relations in the Arkansas, I long to hear of their conversion. Let us not neglect to pray for them daily; particularly, for brother W. The Lord I hope will renew his heart, and make him abundantly useful to the cause of missions.

We rejoice to see brother A. once more in our dwellings. After a long journey from the Arkansas country, he arrived here much fatigued, in the latter part of November. He intends to spend a few months with us, and then return with sister Susan. I do not feel very well about her going into the wilderness, and far from Christian society, where she will perhaps have no religious instruction.

Her mother has removed thirty or forty miles from the missionary station [at Dwight.] But we commend her into the hands of the Almighty, who is able to keep her from evil, and from all the temptations of this delusive world. I am glad to hear from our relations in that country. Brother Walter was expecting to set out in a few days for the city of Washington, and had thoughts of visiting some of the Northern States before he returned. It is likely you may see him in New England. He has placed brother Edmund in the missionary school at Dwight, to continue three or four years. He has become very steady and attentive to his books. I hope the Lord will give him a new heart, and prepare him for usefulness.

Brother W. has given up trading, and has commenced farming. He has purchased land in the Osage country, at the Salt Springs. Whether he intends removing his family to that place, I know not. It is my prayer, that he may brought to bow to the scepter of King Jesus, in whom is life everlasting. As for our going to the Arkansas, it is not decided. Perhaps we shall know better, when your return. You know mother is always very anxious to remove to that country; but father is not. For my own part, I feel willing to do whatever is duty, and the will of our parents. I feel willing to go or stay. The Lord will direct all things right, and in him may we put our trust.

We had the pleasure of seeing your schoolmates McKee and Israel Folsom. They called on us on their way to the Choctaw nation. They said there were many good people at the north. They had rather live among the Yankees, than any other people. I hope they will be very useful to their nation.

Mr. Potter has gone to Brainerd on some business, and I shall stay with Mrs. P. until he returns. We expect him home this week. I hope he will bring a large packet of letters from our Brainerd friends. Mrs. P. is engaged in teaching school while her husband is absent. Several of the scholars are very attentive, and make good progress in their studies. Sarah is in the first Class. She is a good girl to learn, and is much beloved by her teacher. She has begun to read the Bible in course, and has read partly through the

Memoirs of Miss Caroline Smelt. When I wrote to you last, I was in a declining state of health, and for that reason I left my studies to have more exercise. The Lord has been pleased to restore me to my usual health, and I now feel pretty well.

I spent two months in Huntsville last spring, in the family of Dr. Campbell. Mrs.—is a very pious and engaged Christian. I became acquainted with several pious families in Huntsville, who, I believe, feel interested in the cause of missions. The pious ladies made up clothing for the children in Creek-Path. We hope this is only the beginning of a missionary spirit in that place.

I am glad to tell you, that our Female Society is growing in its numbers. We have collected nearly double the sum this year that we did last. The Society has concluded to send our money for this year to the Arkansas mission.

I am glad the people are so willing to assist in advancing the Redeemer's kingdom in our heathen land. May the glorious period soon arrive, when all the nations of the earth shall be brought to the knowledge of the truth as it is in Jesus. Oh, dear brother, though we are widely separated in person yet we are near in spirit, and can unite our prayers for the approach of this happy day.

O let us do with our might what our hands find

to do. I am now in my little study. I have spent in this room many happy hours in prayer to my Heavenly Father. But Oh, how cold and stupid my heart is! How little I feel for the salvation of souls!

> Oh, for a closer walk with God,
> A calm and heavenly frame;
> And light to shine upon the road,
> That leads me to the Lamb.

Please to write soon, and tell me everything respecting your present situation.

CATHARINE BROWN.

TO THE SAME
Brainerd, Feb. 10, 1823.

My dear brother David,

I am at Brainerd, on a visit from Creek-Path. My heart is filled with gratitude to God, in being permitted to see these dear missionaries once more, and unite with them in praise to our Lord and Savior. If feel truly attached to Brainerd, where I first found the Savior; and O how I love the dear sisters, with whom I have spent many happy hours, both in school, and in walking to the house of worship. But those happy hours are past. We must be contented and look forward to that day when we shall meet to part no more.

I left home last week, in company with Mr. Boudinot, and sister Susan. Hope my journey will be beneficial to my health. If our dear father and mother are willing, I indent to pursue study again, as soon as I return home.

There is some seriousness among the people in our neighborhood. Several are very anxious to receive religious instruction. When I return, I think I shall make it my business to go round, once in two weeks, to read and explain the Scriptures to the females.

I cannot but hope the Lord will continue to have mercy on our people, and will bring many to the knowledge of the truth as it is in Jesus.

I hope you will write to our dear parents soon. They are always happy to hear from you.

From your affectionate sister
CATHARINE BROWN.

CHAPTER 5.
HER SICKNESS AND DEATH

After Catharine returned from Brainerd, she seems generally to have considered her removal from the world as not very distant, and to have spent much time in reflecting on death and its consequences. These subjects she not infrequently made the topics of conversation. An instance of this kind is described by Mrs. Potter:

"Entering her room one evening, at an early hour, I found she had retired with unusual debility. She requested me to read, from some medical author, the symptoms of consumption. I complied; and, after comparing them with her own she expressed a belief, she had that disease. I inquired what were her feelings in view of this conclusion. She replied, with tears, 'I am not prepared to die.' You have a hope, I said of happiness beyond the grave? 'Yes, I have a hope resting on the promises of the Savior; but I have been unfaithful!'

"We were both too much affected to say more, and remained for some time silent. At length Catharine sweetly raised her voice, and said 'Sister Potter how beautiful is this hymn;' and then she repeated.

> Why should we start, and fear to die!
>   What timorous worms we mortals are!
> Death is the gate of endless joy,
>   And yet we dread to enter there.
>
> The pains, and groans, and dying strife
>   Fright our approaching souls away,
> Still we shrink back again to life,
>   Fond of our prison and our clay.
>
> Oh, if my Lord would come and meet,
>   My soul should stretch her wings in haste;
> Fly fearless through death's iron gate,
>   Nor feel the terrors as she passed.
>
> Jesus can make a dying bed
>   Feel soft as downy pillows are,
> While on his breast I lean my head,
>   And breathe my life out sweetly there.

"I inquired if she could adopt this as the language of her heart, and she answered with great meekness, that she hoped she could."

It does not appear, that after this her mind was again seriously disturbed by apprehensions respecting *her own* future well being.

But when she saw her aged parents in an infirm state of health, and needing all the attention of an affectionate daughter, and when, moreover, she reflected how many of her dear people remained ignorant of the only Savior of sinners, she clung to life, and her earnest prayer was that she might recover. We are informed that her trials from these sources were, at one time, very severe.

She said to a beloved friend, "I know, that is my duty to submit entirely to the will of God. He can carry on his work without me. He can take care of my parents. Yet I am anxious to recover. I wish to labor more for my people."

How strong her desires were for the improvement of her people, is further evident from this fact, that though David was the only surviving brother, who had the same mother with herself, and though he was dearer to her than anyone else except her parents, she was for some time, unwilling he should be informed of her sickness, lest he should be induced to leave his studies, and come home and see her. Much as she loved him, she said she had rather he would remain in New England, until he was prepared to preach Christ to his countrymen.

In April she was visited by that kind friend of herself and family, Dr. Campbell. He strongly advised, that she should remove to his house, thinking it probable that he might then relieve her.

Her friends all consented, only desiring her to remain at home a few days, till the departure of her brother Webber, who had come from the Arkansas. But his stay was unexpectedly prolonged a month. During this time, Catharine failed so rapidly, that she was unable to ride to Limestone, where Dr. Campbell then resided.

On this occasion, Catharine thus rote to Mrs. Campbell.

Creek-Path, April 17, 1823.

My dear Mrs. Campbell,

My heart was made truly glad this morning, by the arrival of Dr. Campbell. I have long been very anxious to see him, on account of the low state of my health. For two months past it has been declining, and I am now reduced to extreme debility. The affliction I view as coming from my Heavenly Father. I deserve correction, and hope to bear the chastising rod with humble submission.

I have a wish to recover, that I may be useful to my poor countrymen, but know that all human means will be ineffectual without the blessing of God. I pray that Dr. Campbell may be the instrument in his hands of restoring me to health. If the weather were pleasant, I should be disposed to return with him.

I thank you for your present, and wish I had

something valuable to send in return. Dr. Campbell will hand you a little riband. When you wear it, remember Catharine.

Mrs. P. sends love, and hopes to receive a visit from you 'ere long. Much love to the children.

Farewell, my friend, my sister. May heaven grant you its choicest blessings, and reward you an hundred fold for all your kindness to me.— Again I say, farewell. May we meet in Heaven.
Yours affectionately.
CATHARINE BROWN.

As she approached nearer to eternity, her faith evidently grew stronger, and she became more and more able cheerfully to resign, not only herself, but her parents, her friends, her people, her all, to the disposal of her Lord.

May 15th, she was reduced very low by a hemorrhage from the lungs, and for a few days was viewed as upon the borders of the grave.

Before this alarming symptom, it had been proposed to send again for Dr. Campbell. But her parents were persuaded first to try the skill of some Indian practitioners. Their prescriptions were followed, until the hemorrhage occurred. Then her alarmed parents sent immediately for Mr. Potter, hoping he could do something to relieve their darling child. Providentially the Rev. Reynolds Bascom, of whom mention has been already made, had just arrived from the Choctaw nation, on his way to the northern states; and having been afflicted in a similar manner himself, he was able to administer effectual remedies.

It is gratifying to be able to insert her the notices, which Mr. Bascom made, at the time, respecting his interview with her, in this hour of trial.

"May 15. Rode to Mr. Potter's before breakfast. Soon after our arrival, a message came, that Catharine Brown had been taken with bleeding at the lungs, and Mr. Potter was requested to visit her. We accordingly rode over to her father's house immediately after breakfast, and found her entirely prostrated by a copious hemorrhage. After bleeding her in the arm she experienced a sensible relief.

" 16. Visited Catharine, with Mr. Potter, and found it necessary to bleed her again. Conversed and prayed with her, and left her in a peaceful frame of mind

" 19. Left Creek-Path for Brainerd. Mr. Potter rode with us to Mr. Brown's. Catharine appeared sweetly composed. Her countenance was cheerful, and her soul filled with tenderness and filial trust in God. After conversation and prayer, I asked her what she would have me say to her brother David.

"She replied, 'Tell him not to be uneasy about

me. If I do not meet him in this world, I hope to meet him in heaven. I have a great desire to see him, but the Lord may not permit us to meet here.'

"These words were spoken in a low, but audible whisper, and with the significant emphasis of a heart filled with faith and love.

"I have rarely, if ever, seen a more lovely object for the pencil, than she appeared to me on her dying bed. The natural mildness of her features seemed lighted with a beam of heavenly hope, and her whole aspect was that of a mature Christian, waiting with filial patience, the welcome summons to the presence of her Lord."

Mrs. Potter says,—"Death was now disarmed of his terrors. She could look into the grave without alarm. She confessed her sins with great meekness, and mourned that she had not been more faithful in the service of God; yet rejoiced to resign her soul into the hands of her Redeemer.

"Once, when I visited her, she affectionately took my hand and said,— 'My dear sister, I have been wishing to see you, for several days. I have thought a great deal of you and Mr. P. I love you much, but am going to leave you. I think I shall not live long. You have done much for me. I thank you, and hope the Lord will reward you. I am willing to die, if it be the will of God. I know that I have experienced his love. I have no desire to live in this world, but to do good. But God can carry on his work without me. I hope you will continue the meetings of females. You must not be discouraged. I thought when I should get to the Arkansas, I would form a society among the females, like ours. But I shall never live to get there. I feel for my dear parents, but the Lord will take care of them.'

"At another interview she said,— 'I feel perfectly resigned to the will of God. I know he will do right with his children. I thank God that I am entirely in his hands. I feel willing to live, or die, as he thinks best. My only wish is, that he may be glorified. I hope, should I ever recover, I shall be more faithful in the cause of Christ, than I have ever been.'"

A request was sent to Dr. Campbell to visit her as soon as possible. But he was unable to come till the 21st, by which time Catharine was so much enfeebled, as to be entirely confined to her room. She could not ever raise herself without assistance.

The physician gave it as his opinion, that she could live but a few days, unless she was removed to Limestone, it being impossible for him to attend on her at so great a distance. Whether such a removal was practicable, was at first doubted. But a kind Providence furnished unexpectedly such facilities for the measure, that it was determined on.

Before entering on and account of her removal, some further notices of the state of her mind will be given.

Just before her leaving home, she requested a friend to write thus, on her behalf, to her brother David.

"I am entirely resigned to the will of God, and hope you will feel the same resignation. I am perfectly willing to die, or to live, as the Lord shall direct. This world is nothing but sin. I have no wish to live in it but to do good. If it be the Lord's will to take me now, I am willing to go."

Dr. Campbell says;— "Religious confidence and tranquility were at this time her sweet companions. How happy she seemed in my view, so near the confines of the eternal world, about to relinquish all earthly cares and sorrows for the enjoyment of her dear Redeemer's presence.

"On the 23d, she seemed to have the most cheering evidence of her interest in the Lord Jesus. Thus she exclaimed,— 'Now I am ready to die. Oh, how delightful is the view of my Savior! How happy shall I be, when I arrive at my Father's house.'

"On being asked, what would be her feelings, if it was the will of God she should live, she replied; 'The Lord's will be done, and not mine. If I can promote his cause in any way, I am desirous to live. But if I am taken away, I hope my brother David will be useful, in bringing our benighted nation to a knowledge of Jesus.'

"Her soul appeared full, and more than full, of love to God. She spoke much of his goodness to her, and expressed much regret, that she had done so little in his cause. The day preceding this, she had expressed a wish to go to Huntsville, and unite with Mrs. L. and C. in forming an association for prayer, and in endeavoring to do something for the cause of Christ."

Catharine was now unable to endure the motion of a carriage, even for a short distance. It was necessary, therefore, in proceeding to Limestone, to carry her on a litter to the Tennessee river, which was six miles distant; then to take her in a boat down the river, forty miles, to a village named Trianna; and from thence, on a litter again, about five miles, to Dr. Campbell's. But, in order to the successful prosecution of this enterprise, the aid of some person, through the whole distance, who was acquainted with the English language, was indispensable. And it should be thankfully noted, that, just when the question of removal was agitated, Mr. William Leech, a pious acquaintance from Huntsville, providentially arrived at Cree-Path and very kindly tendered his services.

Monday, the 26th of May, was the time

appointed for commencing the journey. Her people then manifested strong proofs of affection and respect.

"Numbers," says Mrs. Potter, "assembled to take, as they feared, and as it proved, a last look of their beloved friend. After a prayer in which she was commended to the divine protection, the canoe was announced to be in readiness, and we followed the litter, borne by her affectionate people, to the river. Old and young were bathed in tears, and some were obliged to use their influence to prevent a general and loud lamentation. Catharine alone was clam, while she bade farewell to those she tenderly loved.

Mr. Leech says, that, "small groups of her acquaintance were frequently seen on the road, waiting her approach. When she arrived where they were, they would hasten to the side of the litter, take her by the hand, and often walk away without speaking a word, the tears all the while rolling down their cheeks."

From Mr. Leech's narrative of the voyage and journey, further extracts will be given.

"About 4 o'clock P.M. on the 26th, we began to glide quite pleasantly down the stream, accompanied by several of Catharine's relatives. Our design was to stop as soon as it became dark, until the moon arose. But we could discover no suitable place for landing, till daylight was gone, and then the difficulty was increased. The margin of the river was generally covered with brushwood. In some places, the shore was a deep mire; at other, there were bluffs and rocks.—This made landing difficult and dangerous in the dark; and along this part of the river were scarcely any settlements.

"At length the danger of running was such, as to determine us to get upon the land in some way. We accordingly steered towards the shore, and providentially discovered a good landing place near which was also a house, where our party was kindly entertained, and our various wants supplied. Had we passed this place, we should not have found such another, for twenty miles.

"When the moon was sufficiently risen, we again started. The night was beautiful, and the rocks and mountains, towering up from the river's brink, looked grand, by the moonlight, as we passed along. The next day the heat of the sun was excessive, and we did not reach Trianna till one o'clock in the afternoon.

"Here we were all strangers. I had, however, a letter from Dr. Campbell to a young gentleman, which I delivered. He obtained a carriage, but Catharine was too weak to ride in it. How to procure people enough, in this land of strangers, to carry her on a litter to Dr. C.'s, a distance of five miles, I knew not. But our situation becoming known, men were soon at hand to carry her, free of all expense.

"And here I would observe, that every person, who saw her, was, so far as I could discover, much interested in her behalf.

"When we were ready to start, our young friend, to whom I brought the letter, placed the mother and sister of Catharine in the carriage, and went himself with them. Thus we were assisted on our way, the Lord putting it into the hearts of strangers to afford us every facility in their power, and we arrived at Dr. Campbell's, a little before dark on the 27th."

Here, not less than at her father's house, she found friends, who were ready to make any sacrifice for her comfort, and with whom she could freely converse on the subject, which lay nearest her heart. Under the skilful care of Dr. Campbell, she soon began to amend, and hopes we entertained, that she would even partially recover.

Early in June, her dear friend, Mrs. Potter, came from Creek-Path to see her. This lady, in a letter to the corresponding Secretary of the American Board, says:

"She then seemed to think she might recover; but manifested no wish to live, unless it should be for the glory of God. She said, 'When I enjoy the presence of the Savior, I long to be gone.'

"While at Dr. Campbell's, I wrote a letter to her brother David, informing him of her illness. When about to close the letter, I went to her bedside, and said, 'Catharine, what shall I say to your brother for you?'"

"After a short pause, she replied, 'If you will write, I will dictate a short letter.'

"Then raising herself in the bed, and wiping a tear that was falling from her eye, she, with a sweet smile, began to relate what God had done for her soul while upon that sick bed.

"To my partial eye, she was, at that moment an interesting spectacle, and I have often wished, that her portrait could then have been taken. Her countenance was softened with the affectionate remembrance of an endeared brother, her cheek was a little flushed with the exertion of speaking, her eye beamed with spiritual joy, and a heavenly smile animated the whole scene. I shall never forget it, nor the words she then whispered in my ear."

The reader will naturally desire to see the letter, which was dictated and penned under circumstances so interesting. It was written in exact accordance with her dictation, and was as follows.

Limestone, June 13, 1823.

My dear Brother,

Mrs. Potter has told you the particulars of my illness. I will only tell you what I have experienced on my sick-bed.

I have found that it is good for me to be afflicted. The Savior is very precious to me. I often enjoy his presence, and I long to be where I can enjoy it without sin. I have indeed been brought very low, and did not expect to live until this time. But I have had joy, such as I never experienced before. I longed to be gone; was ready to die at any moment.

I love you very much, and it would be a great happiness to me to see you again in this world. Yet I don't know that I shall. God only knows. We must submit to his will. We know that if we never meet again in this world, the Lord has prepared a place in his heavenly kingdom, where I trust we shall meet, never to part. We ought to be thankful for what he has done for us. If he had not sent us the Gospel, we should have died without any knowledge of the Savior.

You must not be grieved, when you hear of my illness. You must remember, that this world is not our home, that we must all die soon.

I am here under the care of Dr. Campbell, and his very kind family. My mother, and sister Susan are with me. Since I came here, I have been a great deal better, and the doctor sometimes gives encouragement of my getting well. But we cannot tell. I am willing to submit myself to the will of God. I am willing to die, or live, as he sees best.

I know I am his. He has bought me with his blood, and I do not wish to have any will but his. He is good, and can do nothing wrong. I trust if he spares my life, he will enable me to be faithful to his cause. I have no desire to live in this world, but to be engaged in his service.

It was my intention to instruct the people more than I had done, when I returned from Brainerd; but when I got home, I was not able to do it.

It was a great trial to me not to be able to visit our neighbors, and instruct them. But I feel that it is all right. It is my prayer that you may be useful, and I hope the Lord *will* make you useful to our poor people.

From your affectionate sister
CATHARINE.

How much soever her hopes and those of her friends were raised at this period, with respect to her recovery, they were of brief duration. Though every attention, which an unwearied kindness could bestow, was given her, and prayer was offered continually on her behalf, her Lord and Master was pleased to hasten her departure. She had entered the last six weeks of her life, and thenceforward her descent towards the grave was regular and unremitted.

Dr. Campbell now thought it his duty to inform her parents, and herself, that his hopes, even of her partial recovery, were gone.

Upon communicating this intelligence to her father, who a little before had come to Limestone, the good old man, after a solemn silence of several minutes, observed: "The Lord has been good to give me such a child, and he has a right to take her when he thinks best. But though it is my duty to give her up, it is hard to part with her."

Catharine received the notice without manifesting any alarm. She only requested the doctor to inform her, how long she might probably live.

On the morning of July 17th, she was supposed to have commenced her last agonies, and Dr. Campbell was immediately called to her bedside.

He says,—"I found some appearance of anxiety on her countenance, which was the result of new sensations of bodily distress, and not of any agitation of mind. As soon as she could speak, (for she was sometimes speechless,) extending her hand to me, she calmly observed, 'I am gone.'

"Some hours after this, when her distress returned, and her respiration become very difficult and painful, she said, in reference to her sufferings, 'What shall I do?" I enquired, if, in this trying hour, she could not confidently rely on her Savior? She answered, 'Yes.'

"Through the day her mind was perfectly tranquil, and though several times, when her mother and friends were weeping about her, the tears would start in her eyes, she would quickly suppress them. She seemed to spend most of the time in prayer.

"The night was one of considerable distress, owing to her difficulty of breathing. In the morning she looked toward the window, and asked me if it was not day, I replied that it was. She then turned her eyes towards heaven, and an indescribable placidness spread over her countenance.

"Perhaps she thought, that the next morning she should behold, would be the morning of the resurrection.

"As death advanced, and the powers of nature gave way, she frequently offered her hand to the friends around her bed. Her mother and sister weeping over her, she looked steadily at the former, for a short time, filial love beaming from her eyes; and then,—she closed them in the sleep of death.

"She expired without a groan, or a struggle. Even those around the bed scarcely knew, that the last breath had left her, until I informed them she was gone.

"Thus fell asleep this lovely saint, a little past 6 o'clock, on the morning of July 18th, 1823."

Her afflicted relatives conveyed her remains to Creek-Path, where, on the 20th, they were deposited near the residence of her parents, and by the side of her brother John, who had died about a year and a half before, in the triumphs of the same faith.

Her age was about twenty-three: and six years had elapsed from her first entering the school at Brainerd. She was then a heathen. But she became enlightened and sanctified, through the instrumentality of the Gospel of Jesus, preached to her by the missionaries of the cross; and her end was glorious.

A neat monument of wood, erected by her bereaved relatives, covers the grave where she was laid. And though, a few years hence, this monument may no longer exist to mark the spot where she slumbers, yet shall her dust be preserved in the eyes of the Lord, and her virtues shall be told for a memorial of her.

CHAPTER 6.
HER CHARACTER

A summary view will now be taken of the character of Catharine Brown, as it is exhibited in the documents, which have been the basis of the preceding memoir.

I. HER MENTAL CHARACTERISTICS.

The mind of Catharine was of a delicate texture, well proportioned, and happily balanced. Its perception was clear, its judgment correct, and it was well endued with that invaluable equality in the intellectual economy, good sense. In the acquisition of knowledge, it moved easily, and, considering her circumstances and health, wrought with success. In communicating to others what she knew, she had, owing to the clearness of her apprehensions, more than common felicity.

And who has not remarked her delicate sensibility, her exact views of dignity and propriety, her high principles of action, and her gentleness and sweetness of manner? With her advantages of person, and her excellencies of mind, she needed only greater opportunities, to have attained that high degree of refinement and grace, which is so much admired in the more elegant portion of civilized society.

But, until she came to the age, at which the females of our nation have nearly or quite, completed their education, she derived no benefit whatever from the perusal of books, and enjoyed very little intercourse with civilized people. Her mind, like the wilderness in which she had her home, was uncultivated. But a small degree of intellectual, and scarcely any moral truth, had enlightened it. Bacon, and Newton, and Locke, and St. Paul, and a multitude of others possessing powerful intellects, who had brought the grandest truths in the natural and moral worlds within the comprehension of infantile genius, had, so far as she was concerned, lived in vain. In short, even at that late period, she had almost everything to learn.

She lived but six years after her admission to the school at Brainerd. A desire for knowledge evidently brought her there; and the same desire, strengthened and sanctified by grace, attended her through life.

II. HER ATTAINMENTS.

1. Concerning those attainments, which are *not of a moral nature,* it will be needless to enter into a lengthened specification. It may, indeed, be impossible for us, into whose minds knowledge has been industriously poured from our earliest years, to form a just conception of her intellectual state, before she had access to the ordinary sources of information, or to ascertain, with precision, what revolutions occurred in her apprehensions of things. But there can be no doubt that most, even of the elements of learning, came before her in the garb of novelty, and that the field of her vision expanded, till she at length found herself introduced into quite a different sphere, from that, which had interested the curiosity of her opening youth.

It is affecting to think of the great mental changes, which were necessary, even to place her on a level with the ordinary intelligence of civilized life. But it is delightful to contemplate these changes as more than accomplished. To a few of the more important of them the attention of the reader is, for a moment, invited.

Her acquaintance with the *geographical features of the earth,* before her introduction to the missionaries at Brainerd, must have been exceedingly vague and limited, hardly reaching beyond the wilderness, that embosomed her father's house. Afterwards, that acquaintance was extended to the great natural divisions of the world, its physical aspect, and its civil departments.

Her *astronomical* views, untutored as she was, may easily be conjectured. But she was instructed to contemplate worlds and suns and systems in uncounted numbers, wheeling at the command of their Creator, through immensity.

Her apprehensions respecting the *human race* were so imperfect, that she supposed her own people a distinct order of beings. But soon she learns, that God "hath made of one blood all nations of men."

How exceedingly confined, also, how next to nothing, must have been her knowledge of *history*. Ages that were past, must have been to her almost as much a blank, as ages that were to come. But soon the Bible, the wisest, most sure, most comprehensive history of man, is placed in her hands; and she has besides, access to a variety of the most useful human compends. Being thus favored, it may well be presumed, that the more interesting events of antiquity rose, in rapid succession, above her mental horizon.

Such changes as these elevate the mind immeasurably above the standard of the mere child of nature, and when beheld in any human soul, must be, to a philanthropist, a subject of grateful contemplation.

2. The greatest and infinitely the most important acquisitions of Catharine, however, had respect to *moral* subjects,—to God, and a future state, to the character, duty and highest interest of man, and the provisions made for his salvation. On al subjects of this class, her ideas, when she came to Brainerd, were very confused and imperfect; and in regard to some of the most momentous of them, she was in total ignorance. Scarcely a ray of moral light had gleamed upon her soul. The visible creation was indeed open and bright before her. But how little of the divine perfections does fallen man discern there, until they are pointed out by the finger of revelation!

Of the *moral perfections of God* such as his holiness, justice, and goodness, she had no conceptions at all, when she entered the mission school. Her knowledge of God, like that of most of her countrymen, was confined almost to the narrowest possible limits. *Galunlahtiahi,* or *the Great Being above,* was thought to possess a material form, and his most prominent attribute to be physical strength. The spirituality of Jehovah, his holy character, his love of holiness, his hatred of sin, the strictness of his law, his righteous government over the world, and his illimitable benevolence, were things of which Catharine knew little or nothing.

But soon we find her mind richly furnished with all these views of God. His moral perfections arrest her attention, and she sees, in all their exhibitions, a lovely and attractive glory. What new views of the Eternal must they have been, which drew forth such language as this: — "O, he is good, kind, merciful." "I feel it is good to be afflicted, knowing that the Lord is good, and will always do what is right." "The Lord's will be done, and not mine." "O happy day, when God himself shall be my joy!" No heathen ever used such language as this. It springs only from the illuminations of Christianity.

Of the *Lord Jesus Christ* she had no knowledge, when introduced to the missionaries; and when told of him, for the first time, she supposed that what he had done for sinners had no reference to her, or her people.

But the united testimony of all is, that after her conversion, the SAVIOR was her favorite theme of contemplation and discourse. He was her ALPHA and OMEGA, her ALL IN ALL. Her person, character, and work, appeared to her amazingly interesting. How often does she express a desire to know him better, to love him more, to be more grateful for what he has done, to do more in return, to be with him, to see him, and to sing his praises. "O," she exclaims, "how delightful is the view of my Savior." "He is precious to me. I often enjoy his presence. I long to be where I can enjoy him without sin." "He has bought me with his blood, and I wish not to have any will of my own. He is good, and can do nothing wrong."

And what new views did she acquire, with regard to the people of God. At first, she thought them unhappy, and was fearful they would render her unhappy. But soon she thinks them the happiest people in the world, and longs for their society more than for that of any others. With them she wishes to live, with them to die, with them to be forever. What amount of earthly good would have induced her to forego their company for a single year, and cast her lot among the giddy sons and daughters of fashionable pleasure? "O, happy day," she once exclaimed, in view of approaching death, "when I shall see all the Christians, who have ever lived."

We also perceive a great alteration in her views of *herself*. She has declared, that when she came to Brainerd, she did not know she was a sinner: and we are informed, that she was vain of her person, vain of her decorations, and satisfied with herself.

Yet what self-abasing views had she, ever after her conversion. "I see nothing," she observes, "to trouble me, but my wicked heart. It appears to me, that the more I wish to serve God, the more I sin. I seem never to have done anything good in the sight of God."

"The most conspicuous trait in her character," says Mrs. Potter, "was humility. Though elevated far above most of her sex around her, her conduct towards them was such as to gain their entire confidence and esteem; nor was it ever said—*'Catharine is proud.'*

"I never could discover, that her vanity was excited by the numerous attentions, which she received from different parts of our country. She received them as paid her for Christ's sake. When presents came, her language was, 'These do not belong to me. I do not deserve them. Many Christians have heard, that I love the Savior, and send me presents on this account. But Oh, I feel ashamed that I live so far from him.'

"She received many letters, some of which were highly complementary; but so far from fostering pride, they always seemed to increase her humility. Once having received a letter full of expressions of the strongest admiration of her character, she was gently cautioned against being lifted up with vanity. The tears started into her eyes, and she replied, that she believed people had formed too high an opinion of her, and that if they knew her personally, their esteem would be diminished.

"She was much distressed, that so many of her letters had been published, and, for a season, it was with difficulty, that we could persuade her to write to her correspondents. 'I suppose,' she said, 'the object at *first* was, to show that an Indian could improve. But two or three letters would have answered this purpose, as well as all I have ever written."*

Mr. Leech says, "I have often seen her in company at Huntsville, and although she was very much caressed, and her society sought, by the most respectable people, yet she always appeared humble. There was nothing about her, that was vain, or assuming. This was not the effect of insensibility to those acts of kindness. She would sometimes say to her particular friends, "I wish I was more worthy of such friendly attentions."

Great forbearance was a consequence of this humility of spirit. Says the lady, who has been often quoted,—"I once heard a person rail at her with much ill nature, because she had not performed a small task, which he requested might be done, but which other engagements forbade at the time. She heard with entire composure, without saying a word, and then, although under no obligation to do the work, she quietly took her seat and performed it."

---

*Her letters were published, by different friends to whom they were addressed, to gratify the laudable curiosity of the community. It is proper to remark, however, that not more than two or three were ever inserted in the publications of the American Board.

Again, what a revolution was effect in her views of *this world.* An Indian's heaven, even when most distinctly apprehended, has fewer points of attraction than the earth. Catharine, on coming to Brainerd, evidently regarded it, when she thought of it at all, as an object remote, obscure, and undefined. Hence her imagination had contemplated whatever is lovely and attractive, as shining for chiefly in this world. If she made any comparisons, they did but deepen the conviction, that earthly objects were most desirable.

But after her conversion, what a change! Her contemplations are elevated to a superior world of realities. She learns of a higher state of existence, designed for the good of the human race; where the inhabitants are all holy, their employments holy, their joys holy; where the disorders and miseries of earth are not known; where "there shall be no more death, neither sorrow, nor crying, neither shall there be any more pain;" and where there is "no need of the sun, neither of the moon, to shine in it, for the glory of God doth lighten it, and the Lamb is the light thereof." Now, her views of the world are changed. The contrast of earthly with heavenly things, and of the creature with God, hath spoiled the glories of the world.

"How vain," she says, "does this world appear in my eyes. It is nothing but vanity and sin."

"Sweet and reviving is the thought, that I am not to continue long in this world, but hope soon to rest in the city of my God." "How happy shall I feel, when I land on the shores of eternal felicity."

To proceed father in this analysis, is unnecessary. Enough has been said to illustrate the changes, which occurred in her apprehensions on moral subjects. She seems to have possessed much of that kind of understanding, which is denominated in the word of God, a "spiritual understanding." She appears to have received a spiritual discernment, which enabled her, by the simple reading of the Scriptures, meditation and prayer, to acquire a knowledge of the hidden glories of spiritual things. Hence, the spiritual world which had been concealed before her conversion, was to her, ever after, a world of beauties, upon which she loved to dwell.

III. CHANGES IN HER AFFECTIONS.

The objects of all human affections, may be divided into two grand classes, which are designated, in the divine work, as *things earthly* and *things heavenly.* The earthly things, are the riches, honors, and pleasures of the world. The heavenly things are, whatever bear the marks of a heavenly origin, or of a heavenly destination; such as God, and holy beings, and sacred truth.

When Catharine first became acquainted with

the missionaries, her affections were resting wholly on the former class of objects. But how much evidence is there, that, before her decease, there was almost an entire transfer of her affections; that they rested almost wholly on heavenly things.

With respect to the general character of her religious affections, it may be remarked, that they were uniformly tender, often lively, but never enthusiastic.

"She never appeared," says Dr. Campbell, "to receive the Christian system of faith otherwise than on the force of evidence, and that evidence drawn from the Bible. The extravagance of feeling, which is the effect chiefly of animal excitement she could not comprehend, but felt satisfied with possessing that holiness of heart, which leads to supreme love to God."

Mrs. Potter declares, that "she was never enthusiastic; yet had seasons of exalted joy, when, to use her own language, 'she felt as though she was in heaven, and was disappointed, when her thoughts returned to earth, and she found herself here!' She had, also, seasons of deep sorrow of heart, when she mourned the hidings of her Savior's countenance, and groaned under the pressure of in-dwelling sin."

Catharine possessed nothing of that stoical insensibility to pleasure, or pain, for which the

Indian character has been considered remarkable. There was never anything in her deportment like unfeeling hardihood. The very reverse of this was true. She had a heart for friendship, for sympathy, for tender emotion. This is apparent in all her writing, and in her whole history; and is amply confirmed by her intimate friend and companion, Mr. Potter, who remarks, "Catharine possessed a heart, that could feel for another's woe, and rejoice in another's prosperity."

To the *Savior*, her love was uncommonly strong, and continued so, in every variety of circumstance. Who has not been impressed with this, while reading her journal, her letters, and her recorded sayings, and while contemplating the events of her life? Love to the Savior was her ruling principle. She knew his voice. She delighted to sit at his feet. She was overwhelmed with wonder at this condescending goodness. She was enraptured at the thought of beholding his face.

Here again Dr. Campbell will be quoted. "The Savior seemed to be continually the anchor of her hope, the source of her constant and greatest happiness, and the object of her most ardent love. With her friends she was at all times communicative and interesting; but when He became the theme of conversation, the faculties of her soul appeared to receive new vigor, and she became doubly interesting. —Every expression showed that she was charmed with the goodness of God in making such provision for fallen, lost man. Although on other subjects she was not generally very animated, her whole soul seemed to feel the importance of this, which produced an earnestness of expression and manner, that constrained those around her to feel its importance too."

Hence she felt, and uniformly manifested, a deep interest in the *cause of Christ.* Especially did she long to have her own people savingly acquainted with the Lord Jesus. For this object chiefly she wished to live. This made her almost unwilling to die. "My heart bleeds for my poor people," was her language; "I am determined to pray for them while God lends me breath."

Her biographer might enlarge upon her dependence upon God which led her beautifully to say, "I am a child, I can do nothing; but in God will I trust, for I know there is no one else to whom I can look for help." He might speak of her tender affection for her friends; of her gratitude for favors shown her; and of her compassion for the world at large. But enough has been said to show, that she possessed much, very much, of the meek and glowing benevolence of the Gospel.

> "Fair spirit, nurs'd in forest wild,
> Where caught thy breast those sacred flames?"

IV. HER CHRISTIAN CONDUCT.

There is no reason to believe, that anything in the conduct of Catharine ever approached to what is denominated immoral. And this is very remarkable, considering her early circumstances. Yet, until she came to Brainerd, she was not religious. She did not lead a life of piety. Till then, the only tendency of her mind, and heart, and conduct, was towards the world. As she neither knew nor loved "those things which are above," so neither did she seek them.

But a change occurred in her objects of pursuit; a revolution took place in the general course and tenor of her life. We find new aims, new plans, new habits of action. "Old things are passed away."

Her *habits of devotion* might well render her an example to others. Not only did she delight to be present in the public assembly, not only did she love to gather little circles of her Cherokee friends for social prayer, but she was constant and earnest in her more private approaches to her God and Savior.

Mrs. Potter observes, "The Bible, was her constant companion. The law of God was her delight and meditation all the day. And I think I may safely say, that no morning or evening passed, during her residence with us (which was considerably more than a year,) when she did not retire to hold communion with her God. At these seasons of devotion, I was not infrequently permitted to be by her side, and listen to the frequent breathings of her soul. In strains of the deepest humility, she confessed her sins, acknowledged her obligations to her Heavenly Father, and with great fervency prayed for complete conformity to the divine will. Her dear people were never forgotten, and her petitions were extended from them to all mankind.

"In the warm seasons of the year, the adjacent woods was the place of her retirement, and there are several spots around our humble mansion, on which I never tread but as upon ground consecrated by the prayers of that lovely saint.

"She not infrequently spent whole days in fasting and prayer. One fine summer's day she had been absent nearly all the forenoon in the woods, and knowing that some intoxicated Indians had passed, I felt anxious for her safety, and sent some of the children in search of her. She returned, expressing much concern that she had caused me so much anxiety; and added, that she was sorry she had not told me of her intention to pass that day, in the mountain, which was but a short distance from the house. I then discovered, to what employments she had devoted the day, and regretted that I had disturbed her."

Her *zeal* was not an irregular, evanescent flame. It was permanent, and always active. How faithful, laborious, and successful she was, with respect to her own family, has been noticed in the preceding memoir. A more kind, attentive, and obliging daughter and sister, than was Catharine Brown, or one more faithfully solicitous for the spiritual good of her relatives, is scarcely to be found, it is believed, in any civilized land.

Nor was she ever unmindful of the duties she owed her people, and she seems to have closely watched for opportunities to do to them good. Indeed, their conversion to God was her favorite object, to which she clung, with unyielding tenacity, through every vicissitude of health and circumstance, down to the hour of her dissolution.

> "Patient she strives,
> By prayer, and by instruction, to arouse
> Reflection in the hearts of those she styles
> Her wretched people. Modest, tender, kind,
> Her words and actions: every vain desire
> Is laid obedient at the feet of Christ.
> And now no more the gaity she seeks
> Of proud apparel; ornaments of gold
> She gladly barters for the plain attire
> Of meek and lowly spirits."*

That there were defects in her Christian character, must be presumed, in the absence of

---

*Traits of the Aborigines of America, pp. 161-62.

Positive proof, from analogy. The best Christians have failings. But what were hers? The materials for this memoir were furnished by a considerable number of persons, who knew her well; and, without seeming to have been conscious of the omission, not one of them has specified a single fault in her character, as a Christian. Mrs. P. has simply said, that she was not entirely free from the inadvertencies of youth. It would seem, therefore, and there is reason to believe it was the fact, that her failings, whatever they might be, were not such as are apt to make a strong impression on the mind.

"Through faith in the Lord Jesus," says the first spiritual guide she ever had, the Rev. Mr. Kingsbury, "she was enabled to bring forth the fruits of righteousness, has left a bright example of the power of divine grace over one who was born in the darkness of heathenism, and is now rejoicing with her Savior."

CONCLUSION.

Such was Catharine Brown, the converted Cherokee. Such, too, were the changes wrought in her, through the blessing of Almighty God on the labors of Missionaries. They, and only they, as the instruments of divine grace, had the formation of her Christian character; and that character, excellent and lovely as it was, resulted from the nature of their instructions. Her expansion of mind, her enlargement of views, her elevated affections, her untiring benevolence, are all to be traced, under God, to her intercourse with them. The glory belongs to God; but the instrumental agency, the effective labor, the subordinate success, were theirs.

In her history, we see how much can be made of the Indian character. Catharine was an Indian. She might have said, as her brother did to thousands, while passing through these States, "Aboriginal blood flows through my veins." True, it was not unmixed; but the same may be affirmed of many others of her people. Her parentage, her early circumstances and education, with a few unimportant exceptions, were like those of the Cherokees generally. She dwelt in the same wilderness, was conversant with the same society, was actuated by the same fears, and hopes, and expectations, and naturally possessed the same traits of character. Yet what did she become! How agreeable as an associate, how affectionate as a friend, how exemplary as a member of the domestic and social circle and of the Christian church, how blameless and lovely in all the walks of life! Her Christian character was esteemed by all who knew her, while she lived, and will bear the strictest scrutiny, now she is dead. To such an excellence may the Indian character attain; for, to such an excellence did it actually attain in her.

And why may it not arrive at the same excellence in other Indians? Are there no other minds among them as susceptible of discipline and culture? no other spirits, that, in the plastic hands of the Divine Agent, can receive as beautiful a conformation? And cannot such minds be so fashioned and adorned, that heavenly grace shall beam as charmingly from them, as it did from hers.

The supposition that she possessed mental and moral capabilities, which are rare among her people, while it adds nothing to our respect for her, does injustice to her nation. In personal attraction, and in universal propriety of manner, she was, undoubtedly, much distinguished. But, in amiableness of disposition, in quickness of apprehension, in intellectual vigor, it is believed there are hundreds of Cherokee youth, who are scarcely less favored.

There have been other converts from among her people, both among the old and the young, in whom similar transformations have been wrought. Her brother John, her aged and venerable parents, and others still might be named. More than fifty Cherokees were added to the church the first year after the decease of Catharine, the great proportion of whom adorn their profession in a manner resembling what we admire in her.

It is hardly possible, indeed, that any of these converts should become so well known to our community, as she was. Circumstances have changed. The novelty of Indian missions is gone. The multiplication of converts diminishes our curiosity respecting individuals. But excellence and worth of character, are none the less real for being unnoticed and unknown.

Here, then, we find encouragement. The success of past efforts has been rich in its nature, and animating in its amount; and the same kind of instruments, increased in number, are still employed, and employed too, upon similar materials. The course of divine grace, moreover, is, in some sense, uniform, like the course of nature; so that what Almighty God has done, in past time, is an earnest and a pledge (circumstance being the same,) of what he will do, in time to come. Upon these accounts, among others, we may cherish raised expectations. Should the enterprise which has commenced so auspiciously, be prosecuted with prudence, zeal, and in the fear of God, we shall not be extravagant, if we look for the general prevalence of pure religion among a people, in the midst of whom, at the breaking up of their long night of paganism, this interesting female shone as a morning star.

The present is emphatically the time for vigorous Christian effort. Probably it is the only time when great success is possible. Various unpropitious causes press heavily upon the poor Indians; and it is believed, that nothing will save them from extinction, as a people, but the general prevalence of true religion. All things else will be vain without this

The position, that civilization must precede Christianity, is so unsupported by facts, is so opposed to all experience, that one would think it could hardly be advanced by enlightened philosophers, or be received by rational Christians. What is civilization? In Pagan and Mohnmedian countries, it is, it ever has been, a state of society where moral excellence is little known, and domestic and social happiness little enjoyed; where man is a lordly tyrant, and woman is a slave. True civilization is found only in Christian countries; and nowhere, but as the *result* of Christianity; of Christianity too, planted in the first instance, by missionary enterprise.

Bring this religion to act strongly upon the Indians. Give them the full enjoyment of Christian ordinances. Then their 'winter will be past, the rain will be over and gone.' Agriculture, art, science, legislation, and literature, the germs of which already appear, will grow in rich luxuriance, and the Indian character will be respected by the nations of the earth.

Let the life of Catharine Brown operate as an appeal to the benevolence of the Christian community. Though dead, she speaks: and oh, let her voice fall with persuasive and irresistible eloquence upon every ear.

Shall her people, of whom, by the purifying and enabling influences of the Gospel, so much can be made, be abandoned in ignorance and woe? Shall beings, who are capable of knowing God, of understanding the grand economy of his grace, of enjoying the imperishable blessings of his salvation, be shut out eternally from such wisdom, and debarred forever from such enjoyment?

Are they not susceptible of whatever is useful, and beautiful, and even sublime, in character? Can they not appreciate, and will they not use the means of Christian civilization, if placed within their reach?

And may we not expect an abundant reward? Nay, have we not already been amply rewarded? To say nothing of the impulse given to the intellect, the industry, and the enterprise, of the nation, to which the subject of this memoir belonged; or of their accelerated progress in legislation and government; or of the amelioration in the habits and manners of their domestic and social life; or of the rudiments of learning imparted to a multitude of children and youth; or of the amount of sacred truth, the only means of conversion and sanctification, instilled into their minds; or of an inheritance in the heavens secured to many souls —to say nothing of all this, were not the holy life and triumphant death of Catharine Brown an ample remuneration for all the labors and expenditures of the mission to her tribe?

Say, ye missionaries of the cross, should ye repent of your self-denying toils, if this had proved your only reward? Say ye churches of the Redeemer, would ye recall her sainted spirit from the skies, if what ye have expended for her nation could be refunded? A thousand worlds would not be worth what you have, through the grace of God, secured to her as is humbly believed, in the regions of the blessed. And when ye, also, stand on the heights of the Zion above, and behold her ransomed spirit 'filled with all the fullness of God" and exulting amid the hosts of heaven, will ye have any regrets for the sacrifices it cost you to send the Gospel to her people?

O let sloth be driven away; let the grasp of avarice be loosed; let benevolence assume the dominion; let a spirit of enterprise be kindled; let the messengers of salvation be quickly sent to every tribe that roams the western wilds.

'The wilderness and the solitary place shall be

glad for them, and the desert shall rejoice and blossom as the rose.'

www.ingramcontent.com/pod-product-compliance
Lightning Source LLC
Chambersburg PA
CBHW061441040426
42450CB00007B/1163